THE BAT IN MY POCKET

"She continued to surprise me with contradictions. She walked like a crab, had the affection of a dog, the intelligence of a monkey, hissed and showed pleasure like a cat, slept like a baby and, unfortunately, remembered like an elephant."

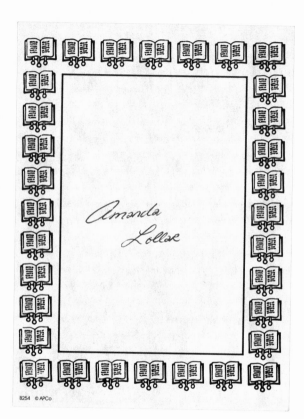

Amanda
Lollar

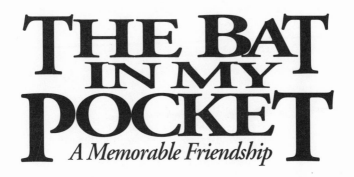

THE BAT IN MY POCKET

A Memorable Friendship

AMANDA LOLLAR

Illustrations by Joann Rounds

CAPRA PRESS
SANTA BARBARA

This book is dedicated to my parents,
Luther and Gladys Lollar.

Special thanks to L. Singh, MD, Dr. Gary Graham, Cherryl Cope, Flint
Immel, DVM, Tad Jarrett, DVM, Terre Wofford, April Toothaker, Susan
Webb, Kitty Cope, Mitzy Lollar, Betty Brooks, Donna Henderson, Mike
Chamberlain, Carlton Robinson, Nellie Garcia, Lori McMinn, Frank Dison,
Lee Shipp, DVM and all of the people at Bat Conservation International.

Illustrations by Joann Rounds.
Cover design by George Delmerico.
Printed by McNaughton & Gunn.

Library of Congress Cataloging-in-Publication Data

Lollar, Amanda, 1955–
    The bat in my pocket : a memorable friendship / Amanda Lollar
    p. cm.
    ISBN 0–88496–347–0 (paper) : $9.95
    1. Bats as pets. 2. Bats—Texas—Mineral Wells—
Anecdotes. 3. Lollar, Amanda, 1955– . I. Title
SF459.B37L65 1992
636′.94—dc20
                                                                    91–37907
                                                                        CIP

C A P R A   P R E S S
Post Office Box 2068, Santa Barbara, CA 93120

INTRODUCTION

THE TRUTH ABOUT BATS is a far cry from popular superstition and mythology. In reality bats are intelligent, attractive animals, and one of man's best friends as well. Some species can gobble up to 600 mosquitoes and other insect pests in an hour; some species have an agent in their saliva that could dissolve blood clots in humans and their guano provides a rich soil nutrient. Tropical bats are important pollinators for many commercially valuable fruits, and aid in seed dispersal and reforestation. Nearly 1000 bat species account for about 25% of all mammals. Contrary to belief, bats are not rodents but are more closely related to monkeys than mice. Fewer than half of 1% contract rabies. Bats are not blind and use high frequency sounds to navigate. This echolocation allows them to avoid something as fine as human hair.

When my bat research began in graduate school twenty-five years ago, I viewed my subjects with intellectual curiosity. I assumed that bats, like other laboratory animals, could be ordered from an animal supply facility. I soon learned that I would need to capture them in their own environment. Those first field trips introduced me to the bat world which I found so fascinating and engrossing that their study became a lifelong commitment.

Amanda Lollar's life was also altered by a chance encounter with a Mexican free-tailed bat. Overcoming her qualms, she endeavored to save the life of a fellow earthling. *The Bat In My Pocket* chronicles Amanda's growing rapport with a mammal that is little understood or appreciated by society at large. Gathering information from limited resources available in Mineral Wells, Texas, Amanda succeeded in bringing Sunshine back to health. Although the bat's wing injury made it a permanent captive, this book stresses that bats should not be kept as pets. As Amanda's reputation as a "bat lady" spread, other injured bats were brought to her for rehabilitation. She soon realized that each of her patients had a distinct and unique personality, which confirms my own observations from over two decades of working with bats. Two Mexican free-tailed bats that I nursed back to health (Tad and Brad from the scientific name *Tadarida brasiliensis*), displayed distinctive behavioral traits, similar to those shown by Sunshine and B.B. in this book.

Amanda's attribution of human characteristics and emotions to her bat friends could be criticized as being too anthropomorphic by some scientists. However, Dr. Donald Griffin, a pioneer in the field of bat echolocation and a member of the National Academy of Sciences, addresses this issue in his book, *The Question of Animal Awareness* (1976). "The possibility that animals have mental experiences is often dismissed as anthropomorphic. . . . But this widespread view itself contains the questionable assumption that human mental experiences are the only kind that can conceivably exist. This belief that mental experiences are a unique attribute of a single species is not only unparsimonious; it is conceited."

Human language is considered essential in the communication of mental experiences. The bats Sunshine and B.B., however, communicated in a variety of ways and taught Amanda to respond to their needs for food, shelter and companionship. This is the heart-warming story of how a bond developed between a human being and an animal in a manner usually reserved for tales of cats and dogs. Sensitivity to the needs and emotions of wild animals is more difficult to achieve. *The Bat In My Pocket* combines a memorable story with accurate information on the biology of bats and their beneficial role in the world's ecosystem.

—Dr. Patricia Brown-Berry
Director, Maturango Museum
Ridgecrest, California; and
Research Biologist,
University of California, Los Angeles

FOREWORD

It's curious what we take for granted, or never even notice. Untold thousands of insects are devoured nightly by our little furry friends, the bats. They emerge at dusk and disappear at dawn, and we are hardly aware of what they have done for us, because the insects they ate never had the chance to bother us in the first place. Try to imagine how it would be without bats. Outdoor barbecues, twilight strolls, evening ball games, and almost every other nocturnal activity would be nearly unbearable unless you were equipped with repellent or a space suit. Now suppose that bats never had a bad rap, but were seen instead as a newly-evolved species capable of bug-proofing our atmosphere in a safe, non-toxic way. Everyone would be abandoning their repellents and space suits and rushing out to buy bat houses to entice winged friends into their yards. This imaginary scene may very well become a reality when we start seeing bats for what they really are—wonderful friends to our world. This book is the story of how it happened to me.

—A.L.

one

Tʜᴇ ʜᴇᴀᴛ ᴡᴀs ᴏᴘᴘʀᴇssɪᴠᴇ the day Sunshine came into my life. I was busy creating a window display for the furniture store my mother and I have in downtown Mineral Wells, Texas and had to interrupt my work to make a bank deposit. I stepped out into the hot sun with my mind still on the window display, paying little attention to my surroundings and almost missed the small furry form on the sidewalk in front of the bank. On closer inspection, I recognized it was a bat.

My first reaction was a shudder of revulsion, but the poor thing was laying on its back, all fours in the air—obviously baking in the heat. Wondering if it was still alive, I nudged it with my foot; the disturbance caused the tiny creature to open its jaws and bare a mouth full of short, sharp teeth. The little animal was scarcely an inch and a half long, and I wondered if it really felt as threatening as it tried to appear.

The bat wasn't pretty to behold, but it was definitely suffering. After gently scooting it onto a newspaper with the toe of my shoe, I went back to the store and found a box for the bat. Then, after filling a jar lid with water, I put the box in the storage room where the bat could stay cool and left it alone to die in peace.

The next day, much to my surprise, the bat was still alive. Assuming it must be hungry and not having a clue what to feed it, I tried apple slices, oats—even a dead roach, and left the offerings in the box. I checked repeatedly but apparently it wasn't the right food or else it was too sick or frightened to eat.

The second day found the creature still clinging to life. I couldn't help admiring its determination to live so I decided to do my best to help it survive and took it home with me. Then, I went to the library in search of information to get this little bat well and on its way. I checked out the only available book on bats. What I learned that day about bats literally changed my life.

It turned out that I had found a female Mexican free-tailed bat; her diet mainly consisted of flying insects—such as moths and mosquitoes. Relieved that she was relatively harmless but still leery, I avoided touching her. Instead, I examined her by moving her gently around with Q-tips and discovered she had an injured wing. She was so weak by then that she hardly resisted, and I realized she needed food as soon as possible.

According to the book, a good diet in captivity was a mixture of equal parts of cream cheese, hard boiled egg yolk, ripe banana, crushed mealworms and a few drops of small animal vitamins. My cupboards held none of the ingredients. No eggs, no banana, definitely no mealworms—whatever they were. All I came up with was some banana nut bread and some cream cheese. After mixing the two together, I offered it to her on the end of a toothpick. She responded immediately and ate it up. Feeling encouraged, I put a glob of the mixture in front of her. She just sat there looking at it, making me wonder what to do next.

I consulted the book again. According to the author, she

would have to be hand-fed. Reluctantly, I picked her up, surprised that she felt so soft and velvety.

Though she seemed reluctant to be handled, she quickly gobbled up the food I offered. This time she spared me her teeth-baring routine. We soon settled into a comfortable position for both of us—her lower jaw resting on the tip of my thumb with my fingers cupped around her back, so she was sitting straight up in my hand. Her little feet straddled and gripped my thumb somewhat like a monkey. She had five toes on each foot and a face that was rather cute at eye level. Her lips were extremely fat with vertical wrinkles and her eyes were small in proportion to the rest of her face. She had a pig-shaped nose and huge ears with potato chip-like ridges completely lining the insides. In my fascination with her face, I didn't watch as closely as I should have while feeding her and, needless to say, food had spilled all over her lips, down her chin and onto her chest.

After she ate her fill, she started slinging her head to shake off the food clinging to her. This accomplished nothing but to spread the food up around her ears and on top of her head. I decided to try my luck with an eyedropper full of water. It was hard to tell when she swallowed, and she wasn't sure how to drink from an eyedropper so now water was all over her along with the spilled food. By the time it was all over, we were both completely stressed out. With relief, I put this sticky, gooey, wet thing that no longer resembled a bat back in the box. Now she looked more like a piece of banana nut bread with feet.

While reading the book, I became more and more fascinated with bats. It seemed just about everything I thought I knew about bats wasn't true at all. Of all the thousand or more species of bats, about seventy percent of them eat bugs. Only three tenths of a percent are vampire bats—limited to South America—and the rest are nectar and fruit eaters. Just one insectivorous bat can eat up to 600 mosquitoes in an hour, and one large colony of Mexican free-tailed bats in Texas can eat a quarter of a million pounds of insects every night. Fruit and nectar-eating bats are among the most important seed dispersers and pollinators of tropical rain forest trees and other plants. Their products include bananas, dates, figs, avocados, mangoes, peaches, cloves and more.

Contrary to popular belief, bats are neither filthy nor likely to transmit diseases. They groom themselves constantly — even more than a cat — and simply cannot stand to be dirty. The poor bat I'd found must have thought I was out to torture her instead of feed her.

Most people believe bats are blind, while in truth they see quite well. Furthermore, they are equipped with a built-in sonar system as sophisticated as anything man has ever invented. They are able to detect obstacles as fine as a thread in total darkness so it's unlikely they would ever get tangled in your hair.

Bats seldom have rabies. Fewer than half of one percent of bats contract rabies, and even those rarely become aggressive. In the early 1950s, researchers made some mistakes about bats. Several bats in these studies had rabies-like symptoms but did not die. From this they gathered that bats were unaffected by rabies and could contract and carry the disease over a widespread area because they would not die of it. It was eventually discovered that the bats they examined had a Rio Bravo type of virus, which isn't harmful to bats or people, but is fatal to mice. The researchers had tested their theory by injecting mice with the bat virus, which, of course, killed them and started the rumor that bats carry rabies.

Another fallacy is that bats only like cold, dark places. They do prefer darkness but still enjoy the sun's warmth. To think I had put the creature I'd found in the coldest place in the store and tried to feed it roaches!

Another interesting note is that bats aren't related to mice or rodents at all. They are of their own order — *Chiroptera*, meaning hand-wing. Bats are actually more closely related to humans than they are to mice. Earlier studies have had them linked to primates — which makes them our distant cousins. Upon learning that bit of information, I began to look at the little bat with newfound respect.

Intent on making her as comfortable as possible, I lined a box with burlap, cut ears off some fuzzy, stuffed animals and sewed them to the sides of the box to simulate bats and, hopefully, make her feel more at home.

She seemed much more comfortable and found a spot right away beside one of the ears. Almost immediately, she started grooming herself — hanging upside down with one foot and combing her fur with the other foot. In no time at all, she looked like a bat again!

Assuming indoor lighting would confuse her nocturnal habits, I placed the box in front of a window so the sun could stream through half of it. With one box flap covering half of the open top and an Afghan placed over the entire box, the sun could filter through, and she still had a dark place to retire for sleeping. She would be able to see the sun go down in the evening and come up each day to keep her body clock right.

Now the bat had everything except a name. Since she was so opposite of everything I had first believed of her, I decided to call her Sunshine.

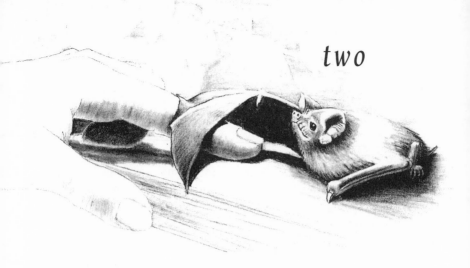

two

Now the problem was mealworms. What are they? Where do they come from? How could I get some? Off to the library I went again. Not much information was available, though I found a photo of one. I called my father to ask if he'd noticed any in an old feed barn he no longer used. Grabbing the box with Sunshine in it, I went over so my dad and I could look for mealworms together.

Luck was on our side. We found quite a few in some old feed sacks with left-over feed in them. Persistence paid off, and we ended up finding about two thousand all together; enough to last the whole winter, if necessary. My father offered one to Sunshine, and she ate greedily. Her face actually took on an expression of utter ecstasy.

Now armed with everything I could find to give her the nutrition her little body needed, I headed back home to make her next meal. As I was driving, I couldn't help but think about how her tiny body had all the same organs as ours—a tiny brain, heart, liver—everything is essentially the same—even the bones in a bat's wings resemble elongated webbed hands. I wondered if her tiny brain feared what her fate might be, and I wished I could somehow communicate to her that I only wanted to help.

In order to keep Sunshine in good health, the mealworms would have to be healthy. The book advised keeping them in a big container full of Wheatena with sliced potatoes for moisture. The laundry room seemed a good place to keep them.

Since I couldn't stand seeing anything suffer, I had a major obstacle to overcome in feeding these living things to Sunshine. It literally sickened me to watch her eat one alive. For days I tried various ways of killing them instantly but nothing worked. They still squirmed in agony and left me so queasy I couldn't eat dinner. Finally, I came up with the idea to freeze them, then thaw them out under running water when needed. The solution worked nicely but had one drawback. When I had to pick out worms from the container, I always felt a little like Hitler.

Sunshine's meals became easier. She seemed to enjoy them much more than the first meal, although she still ended up with a face full of food. At least she would inadvertently eat even more later when she cleaned herself up. She sure was cute when she ate.

At first I only handled her when feeding, but one evening, curiosity urged me into trying to know her better. We both still cringed a little when I touched her or picked her up but the initial fear was gone. Talking to her softly and saying her name, I stroked her small head with my fingertip to see if she would relax. I couldn't help but feel sorry for her, being confined to a cardboard box when she normally had the entire nighttime sky for a playground. And instead of other bats for company, all she had was me—a "giant".

Her wing injury didn't look too serious. A scab was forming on what would be the forearm part of the wing, but that was all I could see so far. The library book stated that any serious break to bat's wings would cause them to go into shock and die rapidly, so I felt sure it wasn't broken anywhere.

Hopefully, it wouldn't take her long to fly again.

Mexican free-tail bats migrate for the winter months, which were coming soon. If Sunshine wasn't able to fly by then, I'd be stuck with her for the winter.

Studying her closely, I was amazed at how she was put together. Her face was almost dog-like, but it showed intelligence like a monkey's. She was so borderline ugly she was cute. With fat little lips and a perpetual grin, she came closer to the resemblance of a troll doll than anything I had ever seen.

Her wings folded up tight and looked like long arms at her sides, extending forward towards her head with a thumb attached at the end. The thumbs were used for climbing and holding onto buildings. Along with her five long toes for gripping, she could climb as well as a monkey. When she walked, she looked like a little crab. All in all, she resembled about five different animals, depending on which angle you looked at her.

She seemed to relax somewhat as she sat in the palm of my hand. I stroked her tiny head and then continued with my finger on down her back. She didn't seem to mind and after a few strokes, her tail started arching up a little more with each touch until it came up each time, much like a cat's when you pet it. I continued petting her head and then rested my finger in front of her nose so she could get used to me further. Her next move left me stunned. She sniffed my fingertip, then moved towards me and laid her wing across the end of my finger in a gesture that seemed to mean acceptance. I tried to find another reason for her action but her move was too purposeful to be anything else. Her small gesture filled me with awe and touched an inner part of me permanently.

It was now very hard to leave Sunshine alone. Each evening, I would get her back out of her box and hold her in the palm of my hand. Eventually, she decided she'd be more comfortable upside down and would turn so her head faced my little finger and her toes gripped my first finger, with her little back against my palm. She seemed to enjoy being like this and would soon drift off to sleep. After a few weeks, she seemed to consider my left hand hers. I must have done the same thing subconsciously because each evening found me doing more and more things with one hand.

At times when both my hands were needed, I would either put her on my shoulder or tuck her into the folds of my sweater and set her on the couch. She loved to look around while perched on my shoulder and would open her mouth slightly, sending off echolocation noises. Most sounds are undetectable to human ears but every once in a while, a slight clicking could be heard. Children's ears are much more sensitive than adults and some can hear the noises bats make. In fact, some of the higher-pitched squeaks from bats can be painful to a child's ears.

When in the folds of the sweater, she would snuggle back with just her face and ears peeking out, looking completely content. From the couch, she could see me in the kitchen and would watch my actions unblinkingly.

I could easily keep an eye on her as well. Eventually, she would tire and just lay her little head down — lowering her ears down over her eyes like a miniature sombrero — and go to sleep. She reminded me of a baby with a blanket pulled up over its shoulders.

One day I made her a tiny blanket just for fun. Setting her on a big throw pillow on the couch I spread the blanket over her. Apparently she didn't feel as secure as she did in the folds of my sweater because she didn't stay put. Finally, she went a little too far and took a tumble off the side of the pillow. Somehow the blanket ended up beneath her. Not being able to grab hold of anything, she clung tight to the blanket with all fours. Down the side of the pillow she rolled, all her limbs stiff in the air and holding the blanket taut until she was a fast little blur of blanket, bat, blanket, bat, blanket, bat. Even though she was headed towards the couch cushion, I quickly rushed to her aid. Picking up her trembling body I tried to calm her through my laughter. Needless to say, she never drew comfort from her little blanket.

The weather was now turning colder and I needed to wear the sweater Sunshine seemed to adore. A replacement she would trust was needed. Using an old black sweatshirt, I made a small rectangular pillow and stuffed it with cotton batting. I then folded the pillow in half and sewed the sides shut, leaving one end open. The whole thing was slightly smaller than a shoebox and resembled a dark fuzzy cave inside. She could go to the back and hide completely if she wanted to, or peer out the opening in the front and still feel secure. Since she was used to being in close contact to bats while roosting, the soft walls surrounding her seemed to give her comfort. I dubbed this invention her "nerf cave."

three

THE WEEKS FLEW BY rapidly and winter was fast approaching. Business was picking up at the store, and there was always a lot to do throughout the day. No matter how busy I was, my mind would repeatedly stray back to Sunshine.

She was so fascinating that each evening I could hardly wait to get her out of her box just to hold and gaze at her. She kept me in rapt entertainment—often an hour or more would go by unnoticed as I watched her captivating actions. Hanging upside down on my hand with one foot and grooming herself with the other foot, she would meticulously comb every inch of her body. She would lick her wing and tail membranes like a cat. Seeing her yawn was almost frightening. Her mouth could open extremely wide —enabling her to catch moths—and she had as many teeth as a dog. Seeing all these teeth in an animal so tiny still made me uncomfortable, and I realized it was only because it was a bat I was looking at. If I were holding a small puppy or kitten in my hand with the same number of teeth, it certainly wouldn't be scary. All three animals were equally as harmless, but old misconceptions die hard. I realized that even in myself, there were still some qualms to conquer.

Riding on my shoulder, between my sweater and sweatshirt, was fast becoming a favorite spot for Sunshine. Her most comfortable position was clinging sideways on the sweatshirt in the area of my collarbone with her nose barely visible in the neck opening of my sweater.

Whenever she sensed some action, little beady eyes and huge ears would appear and if the action was deemed interesting enough, the entire head would slowly emerge, staying until boredom set in.

Interesting actions included walking through the house, reading the paper, folding clothes, and especially going out on the porch in the evening to look for moths. Her entire little body would vibrate in anticipation of the treat. But her joy never diminished my qualms in catching the moths and trying to kill them instantly before offering them to her eager mouth.

Before long, Sunshine was spending most of each day in my hand, on my shoulder or on the couch in her nerf cave. She had such an irresistible personality that I had to admit to myself that, yes, I was actually becoming attached to — of all things — a bat. She must have felt somewhat the same as she no longer tensed up when I picked her up from the box. She now crawled into my hand eagerly, either for company or to be out of the dreaded cardboard box, or maybe just for the warmth of my hand.

Since most bats travel in colonies, she must have hated being so alone. With dread I put her up each night, knowing she would be awake all night long in a box by herself. At times I feared she might die of loneliness since it must have seemed like an eternity to her before she got out of the box again. A few times, she had tried to cling to my fingers when I was putting her up for the night. I'd have to use my other hand to gently pry off her toes from my fingers; but just as soon as I'd get the second foot loose, she'd grab back on with the first foot. Sometimes she hung on so hard that

I felt cruel and ended up staying awake awhile longer with her.

She had yet to make much noise so I had no idea what a bat sounded like. One night, she was determined she was not letting go of my hand. After ten minutes or so of continuously plucking her toes from my fingers, I finally won, only to have her turn around in her box to look up at me so pitifully that tears rolling down her cheeks would not have been surprising. Feeling extremely guilty but determined not to give in, I stroked her tiny head a few times and told her goodnight, quickly closing the lid and trying hard to forget her forlorn image. After a week of staying up late to keep her company, I couldn't wait for my head to hit the pillow.

I wasn't in bed five minutes when she decided to make her first noise, a very definite, high-pitched, loud peep. I waited a minute to see if she would peep again but no sound came. The silence that followed made me wonder if I should answer, so out of curiosity I spoke her name quietly. That was all it took. Knowing she'd been heard, she answered back with a string of loud, constant peeps. Slightly alarmed and kissing my good night's sleep goodbye, I got up to make sure she was all right. As soon as I lifted the box lid, the peeps stopped. When I went to pet her head and tell her goodnight again, she took advantage of the situation and literally jumped into my hand. Little did I know that this was just the beginning of Sunshine taking complete control of my life.

In no time at all, she learned that by peeping, she could get my attention. Every other night or so, she'd go into her peeping routine until I'd pick her up again. There was no way to ignore her. Besides the noise being impossible to shut out, knowing she was actually calling me didn't make me feel any better. Each peep would sound more pitiful until I would feel like a cruel monster, and, of course, give in.

Once in my hand or on my shoulder, the change was dramatic. A contented look would appear on her face as she drifted off to sleep while I stayed awake. How I wished I could sleep as soundly as she. Bats have the ability to enter torpor—a state of greatly reduced metabolism which can lower their body temperature to that of the air around them. Most of the time, the house was kept around seventy degrees. Finding her torpid on several occasions, I actually thought she was dead. Her little body was so cold that she barely moved, the sleep being so deep that it took several minutes for her to be able to function. Vacuum cleaners, television, radio—nothing woke her up during the day. Well, at least one of us was getting some rest.

Staying up with her in my rocking chair, I inevitably fell asleep one night. I woke around two a.m. to find her gone! I turned on the lamp, moving only my arm just in case she was tucked under my body somewhere. The first thing I checked—after myself—was the floor where I was stepping. The next fifteen minutes I spent on my knees, looking in empty suitcases, under the bed, in corners, behind the nightstand, every inch of the dust ruffle, under the chest and finally found her camouflaged beside the leg of my rocking chair, looking right at me with little eyes glittering mischievously. To this day, I still believe she enjoyed watching me crawl around on my hands and knees calling her name over and over almost frantically. Back in her box she went and not a peep did she make. Her escapade must have worn her out. That made two of us.

The next day I devised a plan that I hoped would satisfy both of us. The night stand beside the bed had a deep bottom drawer. After emptying the drawer, I lined the bottom half all the way around with sweatshirt material. More stuffed animal ears were hung on the sides in various places. Then, clear contact paper was stuck into the top half of the drawer all the way around. Newspaper on the bottom of the drawer completed her little nighttime room. The sweat-shirt material was high up enough for her to be in her usual upside down position comfortably and the contact paper was too slick for her to get a toe hold, which prevented her from climbing any higher than the halfway point in the drawer. There was also room for her nerf cave and the whole effect looked cozy.

That night the test began. As soon as I heard her peep from her "new room," I dangled my arm off the side of the bed with my hand just inside the bottom drawer, within Sunshine's reach. She gratefully crawled on and made herself comfortable. There was no worry of her crawling up my arm as I had found out sometime ago that she couldn't get a grip on any smooth skin surface. I settled into blessed sleep knowing she couldn't go anywhere. She seemed quite happy with her new room and emitted soft, contented peeps each night when she found my hand. From then on, when she decided she needed some company, she'd peep until I put her in the drawer and, thankfully, we'd both be happy.

I must have conditioned myself to not close my hand in my sleep, for I never did. Occasionally, she would wake me up by tickling my hand somehow. She must have been playing because it felt like nothing she had done before. I was never able to see what she was doing since she would stop when I turned on the light.

About this time that I began wondering about myself. I didn't have bats in my belfry—yet—but I sure had one in my nightstand. If this was the beginning of my going batty, I had one consoling thought—at least I'd be well rested for it.

four

Sunshine yawning . . .

AFTER SUNSHINE STARTED peeping, she went on to speak the entire bat language. Her different noises seemed to communicate different feelings and needs, and after a few days I began to understand her. A soft chittering noise seemed to convey greeting, affection and happiness. More often than not, she combined the chittering with rubbing her nose softly but vigorously up and down on my finger. The effect was much like a dog happy to see you, licking and nuzzling your hand.

She had a reaction to everything: excitement, boredom, happiness, hunger or affection. All of them could be read on her face, and her chitterings took on different notes to match these emotions. Occasionally I could get her to chitter back to me before I picked her up, just by calling her name.

Another sound she made I dubbed her zipper noise. It resembled the sound a plastic zipper makes if you zip it quickly, stalling about every inch or so. She "zipped" whenever she seemed to question or was unsure of the situation. Although she loved to ride on my shoulder, my bending over or moving too quickly would always cause her to dig her little feet in and "zip-zip" until I was upright or walking normally again. When feeding her, if the food ever stopped its forward motion to her mouth, or didn't arrive fast enough to please her, her whole body would tense up and the zips would start.

Loud peeping seemed to be used only for distress. I learned the hard way that these noisy squeaks while she was on my shoulder or in my hand meant she had to relieve herself. Bats do not like to soil themselves or their roosting area. Tissues became a permanent object in my pocket. She readily moved from my hand to the Kleenex, and then back on my hand when finished, further proving just how clean and intelligent bats really are.

Sunshine was fast becoming aware of the power of her peep. Arriving home in the evening, normally I'd first greet the dogs and pet them. Invariably she would hear my voice from inside her box, and would peep relentlessly until I got her out. There came times during the day when I actually had to tiptoe into my own home, hoping the phone wouldn't ring so she could hear my voice. Then I'd quickly get what I needed and leave before she woke up. This was much easier than hearing her cries and knowing I'd pick her up to comfort her; then I'd have her vise-like toes to fight along with her mournful peeps.

To make matters worse, Sunshine started using her peeping cries when I'd put her up for the day before leaving to open the store. This was once the easiest parting time for both of us, as she was sleepy after her breakfast, and well aware the sun was up.

One particular day I was headed to a furniture auction before going to the store. It was a beautiful 70 degree day—not uncommon during a Texas winter. I was looking forward to the two-hour drive on such a pretty day.

As I was trying to leave, Sunshine once again designated me the cruel giant, while she of course played the part of the abandoned, helpless, tiny fur-ball.

Almost out of range of the painful peeping, suddenly I changed my mind and went back to get her. Her chitterings and squeaks sounded almost ecstatic as I put her under my sweater. Grabbing her nerf cave and a cardboard box, out the door we went. Clinging with her velcro feet and thumbs, she definitely looked pleased, eyes and ears peeking out by the collar of my blouse. Her happy noises continued throughout most of the trip there. As I talked softly and petted her, she would chitter back almost as if in conversation with me.

Although she was trying not to miss any action, sleep was winning her over. Her little sombrero ears would start lowering over her eyes, then suddenly jerk back up, afraid to miss anything. This action repeated itself over and over, until each time the ears stayed down a little longer, and sleep finally won.

Arriving at the auction, sleeping Sunshine was put in her nerf cave, and the cave was placed in the cardboard box so she couldn't climb out if she awoke. Locking the doors secured her in until I returned to find her still asleep.

Sunshine awoke during the trip home and peeped until she was put under my sweater again. She slept all the way back, only waking twice, chittering about something and then falling back to sleep. Back at home she didn't even protest being put in her box, only nuzzling my fingers before falling back to sleep again.

A few evenings later there was a program about bats on television. After watching the bats move about in their roost, I noticed they seemed much more nimble than Sunshine. Perhaps Sunshine's injuries were more serious than I realized. The left side of her body always seemed stiffer, and she seemed to drag the left wing beside her. She may have hit a powerline or something while in flight. I hoped she was only bruised and not something worse. The other bats in this area had left for the winter, so she couldn't be set free until spring, but now I wondered if she would ever fly again.

By this time I was so attached to her that keeping her would actually be a pleasure, despite all the time it took to care for her daily. She had so many human qualities it was like having a tiny person in the house. Although I loved my dogs and cats, they seemed rather boring in comparison.

Every so often I had to stop and be thankful to have this little creature in my life, even if temporarily. I prayed she wouldn't have trouble re-adapting after all these months away from other bats. Not knowing her age made it more difficult. If she had been born the past spring and this was her first summer to fend for herself, she might decide being domestic was much easier. An older bat would have more trouble adapting to captivity. Sunshine must have been fairly young since she adapted so easily. She seemed completely happy with her situation, and her giant slave.

Sunshine was constantly grooming herself, but her fur had begun matting up on the left side of her neck. Closer inspection revealed the fur nearest to the skin being heavily matted. Wondering why she wasn't cleaning this area, I decided to clip the fur to see if she had an injury I wasn't aware of.

Using small manicure scissors and an eyebrow brush, I gently clipped and combed her fur. Sunshine obligingly turned her little head the opposite direction as I clipped, as if she knew not to get in the way. But as I cut into the thickest part of the mat, she proved just how difficult she could be. She squirmed, she peeped, she glowered at me with beady eyes and finally she bit me. Luckily, Mexican free-tailed bats are small, their teeth are very short and their jaws normally aren't strong enough to break the skin when they bite. The whole effect feels like a quick pinch. Bats rarely bite, and this was the first time she had ever offered to bite me so I was mildly shocked. There wasn't an injury underneath, and I wasn't causing her pain. She had bitten me out of anger. The mat was so thick it was doubtful she could comb it out herself as she groomed, so I continued. Finally, after 20 minutes of tedious clipping and combing, the mat was gone and thankfully so was Sunshine's pique.

The fur was short next to her neck now. Running the brush through the fur caused Sunshine to start scratching air, much like a dog does when you scratch a good itchy spot for it. Assuming she'd want to groom her newly exposed fur, I stopped brushing so she could do it herself. Watching her comb her fur with her little foot, I realized why she had become matted in the first place. No matter how hard she tried, she couldn't reach or groom the neck area. She easily groomed her face, ears, and neck on the right side with her right foot, so apparently this was another aspect of the injury to her left side.

She seemed relieved to be rid of the mat, and as I brushed the area again for her she continued to scratch the air, bending her neck this way and that in order to feel it in all the right spots. Satisfied her neck was clean, I decided to brush her head where I assumed she couldn't reach also. This turned out to be something she dearly loved, for each time I tried to stop she'd push her little head up under the brush, chittering and bobbing with her head until I started brushing again. Grooming her became a daily ritual she eagerly looked forward to. Just showing her the brush caused an instant reaction of chittering and pushing her head under the brush. I also looked forward to watching her enjoy it so much, with her eyes half closed in bliss and just chittering away.

Brushing her took us one step further to washing her face and ears with a warm damp cotton swab. This was yet another activity she grew to love and expect daily.

Sunshine now seemed to realize that you could bite the giant and get away with it. She was quick to point out that

I was only allowed to brush her in areas that she couldn't reach herself. When I strayed too far, a quick nip would put me back in my place. I was, however, allowed to wash most of the hairless areas of her body with a cotton swab, like her feet, lower belly, entire face and the outside of her wings. Little did I know I had just completed the early stages of creating a spoiled rotten bat.

five

Having always been an animal lover, dogs and cats have constantly been a part of my life, along with a multitude of strays including pigs, orphan racoons, a pet skunk, and horses. I've always prided myself in having healthy, slightly spoiled but well-behaved animals. Raising and training horses, obedience-training a few dogs, and paper-training my skunk was reason enough for me to believe I'd become a fair judge of animal intelligence over the years. Although no animal expert, I still felt justified in saying that Sunshine was the smartest of any animal I'd ever had, including dogs and cats. But even having this first-hand experience with a bat, I still had a hard time believing that something so tiny could be so intelligent.

Living alone for many years has made me appreciate the company of animals even more, and after a while you even tend to look upon them as your children. Besides Sunshine, the present children included Grunt, a young dog I had found starving and had nursed through Parvo. He had named himself by grunting pitifully nonstop throughout his entire illness. There was also Useless, the stray cat who proved worthy of his name, and Nuisance, another stray whom I found at the store one day with his head stuck in an air vent. After freeing him he decided to never leave me alone again. Last but not least there was Brillo, my little wire-haired mutt and 10 year veteran of all the foster children.

The new foster child was a stray cat who had recently had kittens. While she was gone I was looking over the newborn litter, still with their eyes closed. Sunshine was safely tucked away and sleeping under my sweater when I decided to show a kitten to her.

Putting my hand under my sweater I felt the now familiar sensation of Sunshine climbing onto my fingers. I showed her the kittens from above, then picked up one of the harmless babies and showed it to Sunshine close up. She tensed when she saw it, but felt safe enough to go ahead and sniff it. One smell was all it took. She went completely rigid, opened her mouth wide and actually hissed! I quickly put the kitten down, but not before Sunshine bit me hard and then glared at me with contempt.

The irony of the situation was almost comical. Through most of the day limericks popped uncontrollably into my head about "the bat that hissed at the cat" — almost like one of those inane songs that lodges in your mind.

Sunshine stayed mad at me most of the day. She was her normal affectionate self much of the time, but every once in a while she would bite me for no reason, as if she were remembering the kitten. Immediately after biting me, she would chitter and rub her nose softly in the exact spot she had bitten, as if to say "Sorry for biting you, but you know you deserved it."

She still continued to surprise me with contradictions. She walked like a crab, had the affection of a dog, the intelligence of a monkey, hissed and showed pleasure like a cat, slept like a baby and, unfortunately, remembered like an elephant.

That evening she apparently still hadn't forgotten and decided to give me one last lesson for my thoughtless action. Lately she had taken to exploring under my sweater, and her journeys had taken her into the sleeves, around my back and under the collar flap of my blouse. That evening she discovered that my neck lay just beyond the collar. She was sniffing and nudging the side of my neck while I was trying hard not to cringe at the way it tickled, then all of a sudden she bit me again.

I was almost to the point of being used to getting "put in my place" with her little nips, but the neck area was something else entirely. I quickly plucked her off my collar with images of Dracula crossing my mind. As attached as I was to this lovable little creature, I still felt squeamish and thoroughly ridiculous as I checked my neck for the tell-tale mark. Yet as unnerved as I felt, one look into her endearing little face brought me back to reality.

The subconscious is much harder to defeat. That night I had nightmares about my dear little bat.

six

The New Year had come and gone. By mid-January the mealworm supply had rapidly declined. Still unable to obtain information about mealworms, I was afraid of running out of Sunshine's main food supply.

The remaining mealworms would have to be rationed to her daily. But before they could be rationed, I had to know how many were left, and divide that amount by how many days were left until spring, when she might be able to fly again. Armed with a bucket and a scoop, I sat on the laundryroom floor and began the laborious task of sorting through the grain for mealworms, then dropping them in the bucket to be counted later. The only happy aspect of this task was Sunshine contentedly perched on my shoulder, watching every move intently and occasionally smacking her fat little lips as the bucket slowly filled up.

Texas winters sometimes provide warm enough days for moths to come out at night, and luckily this January was milder than usual. I was able to catch quite a few moths and freeze them ahead also.

Jimmy Davis, a neighbor in his early teens, had been quite fascinated with Sunshine from the beginning. With Jimmy's help, quite a few moths were stockpiled. Each warm evening Jimmy would be across the street under his porch light, and I'd be under mine, both of us purposely swatting at moths. What a sight we must have been to passing motorists, who probably wondered why we didn't just turn off the porch lights.

A few evenings later I reached for Sunshine after I had sliced some avocados. I had rinsed my hands and dried them, but apparently the scent of avocado was still detectable. Sunshine was so captivated by the smell that she stayed put under my sweater, sniffing my fingers instead of eagerly crawling on my hand. Back in the kitchen I cut some avocado into pieces small enough for her to try. The aroma caused her head to peek out of the sweater, nose wiggling like a dog's at the scent.

Sunshine enthusiastically ate the small slivers, barely stopping to swallow. I'd never seen her jaws go quite so fast when eating and she couldn't seem to get enough. Before long she had more in her mouth than she could manage. Pieces of half chewed avocado started coming out the sides of her lips as she tried to gobble even more.

As I made her slow down, I wondered if I had unleashed some kind of monster. She dearly loved avocado, and from then on she would get a small sliver of it for dessert after her meals.

After trying this strange new food she seemed curious to try other culinary delights. Occasionally, during my cooking or eating something, a certain scent would seem to interest her, so I'd offer her bits of everything until she found what she wanted. She would taste anything offered but developed the nasty habit of spitting out unacceptable food. This wouldn't have been so bad if she had done it gently, but as she spit she would sling her head to one side with such force that the food would actually become a small projectile flying across the room. Trying to locate the globs of food as they were airborne wasn't easy and not my idea of an entertaining evening.

Among the foods that never took flight were yogurt, bananas, scrambled eggs, peas, baked potato, macaroni, pimento cheese, tapioca pudding, cottage cheese, ham, baked squash, cream cheese, oatmeal, and health food cookies.

With all these other foods, the worm supply would last longer. By substituting one of the more nutritious foods for worms once in a while, it wouldn't be too unhealthy for her, I reasoned.

Unfortunately Sunshine had the same idea but carried it to the extreme. All she wanted to eat was avocado. Offering her a worm would cause her to clamp her little lips together and turn her head away. The normal pattern of her meals consisted of my trying to get her to eat a worm for about 10 minutes, with her determination only growing stronger with each passing minute. Then as soon as I'd offer her the avocado, it would disappear in a green blur.

Not realizing what she was doing the first time or two, I really didn't worry. But as days passed and she refused worms repeatedly, I knew we had a showdown on our hands. She was an insect eater and needed much more than avocados could offer. Showing her a live worm to eat only caused her to look confused. After three months of eating only dead moths and worms, food that moved was no longer her style. Slightly relieved that she didn't eat it alive, I decided to try rolling a dead worm in avocado. She once again proved her intelligence by eating the avocado off the worm. To make matters worse, I was out of frozen moths and none could be found due to a cold spell.

The last step was just to let her go hungry. I'm sure I suffered as much as she did during our showdown. The hurt look on her face as I put her in her box hungry the first few times almost did me in. Her peeps sounded almost frantic as I closed the box and left her alone. At other times I could swear I'd hear her even as I was pulling out of the driveway in the mornings.

Finally after a few days she gave in. She quickly learned that if she wanted avocado, she'd have to eat a few worms first. Feeling extremely relieved and happy she was eating normally again, I put her in her box once again to leave for the day.

Not a peep did she make as I sat her down and gave her my usual good-bye rub with my fingertip. But as I was rubbing her face, she put her wing against my finger, then pressed my finger to her face and held it there while looking up at me. It was such an affectionate gesture that it almost brought tears to my eyes. She seemed to be saying thank you.

Besides Sunshine unintentionally making her mealworm supply last longer, two other things also helped. While cleaning out another part of the old feed shed, my father found about 500 more mealworms. Then my niece, Mitzy, provided me with some invaluable information. Her junior high school science class had recently been involved in a project of raising mealworms. Her science teacher gave me another 300 mealworms left from the project and, more importantly, told me where I could order more.

seven

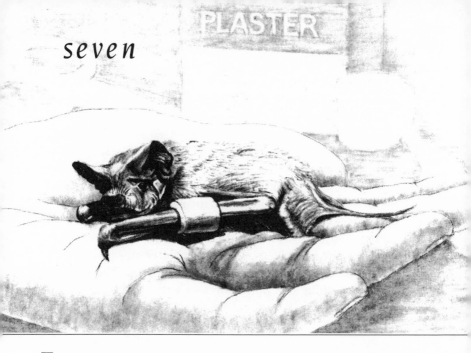

Fᴇʙʀᴜᴀʀʏ ᴛᴜʀɴᴇᴅ ᴏᴜᴛ to be a slow month for the business, and life settled into a less demanding pace. Oftentimes my mother and I would pass the inactive days at the store by reading. Both of our favorites were horror novels—though I now tended to avoid titles such as "Demon Bats."

Sunshine was getting a little easier to put up each morning before I left. Her mournful peeps were getting fewer and farther between as she accepted her fate. However, I still felt heartless each time I closed the lid over her pleading face, even when she wasn't peeping.

On impulse one day I decided to take her with me. Figuring I could put her box in the office and slip her in if necessary, I tucked her under my sweater and off to work we went. Sunshine was so content not to be alone that she quickly fell asleep on my shoulder, and she hardly moved until noon, at times making me forget she was even there.

My mother was also fond of Sunshine, and aware that she had come to work with me. The plan was for her to wait on customers if needed, while I put up Sunshine in case someone else came in that I might have to wait on.

The situation worked out quite well for a few days. Sunshine's antics made time pass a little faster at the store, and Sunshine was much happier. A few times a day she would awaken and peep softly, wanting to come out of the sweater to stretch and groom herself. For this I would either hold her in my hand or put her in the box for a while. My usual post was behind the checkout counter, so she could be concealed quite easily if necessary. I also kept her nerf cave on a shelf by the paper bags under the cash register and slipped her inside when I needed to ring someone up. She seemed to like watching the giants interact with each other—eyes wide with interest, looking up from below. Other giants didn't seem to scare her, but she still remained somewhat shy and reserved around them.

Of course by now I found nothing wrong with carrying a bat around with me, though I was sure other people would have thought me quite strange. Even I would wonder about someone taking their pet mouse or hamster to work with them. Sunshine was nothing like a rodent, although it would be easy to make the comparison. Lots of pet owners take their dogs everywhere with them and of course are considered perfectly normal. Sunshine far surpassed the company of any dog I'd ever had, and even though I found it quite ordinary to take my bat "bye-bye" and enjoy her companionship, I was sure no one else could possibly understand.

Knowing the misconceptions about bats, and that some people even fear them, was yet another reason to keep her hidden.

The day eventually came when I didn't get a chance to put her up before waiting on a customer. Sunshine was sleeping so soundly that I doubted she'd waken and peep, so I left her alone to sleep under my sweater while I helped the unsuspecting soul pick out a comfortable chair in the color she wanted.

As she left she complimented the quality of our furniture and the courtesy we gave our customers. I couldn't help but wonder if she would have felt the same had she known the nice lady waiting on her had a sleeping bat hanging under her sweater — and even liked it there.

More and more I would leave her dozing under my sweater while I waited on people. I realized I was pressing my luck, but it seemed so much easier to just leave her alone to sleep. A few times while talking with someone, I'd feel small movements on my collar bone. Glancing down I'd see Sunshine's tiny head sticking out the edge of my sweater, peeking through and barely concealed by my medium-length hair. She rarely peeped when she heard other giants around, and the few times she did I was able to cover it by clearing my throat.

My niece, Mitzy, who was eleven at the time, fell in love with Sunshine from the start. Often she would come to the store to visit, and thought the whole situation with Sunshine was shockingly funny. My waiting on a customer with Sunshine concealed would put her on the edge of her seat. She would literally hold her breath until the customer left the store.

My mother and I had exhausted our supply of horror books, so I needed to visit our favorite bookstore down the block. Mitzy was there for the day and we both felt particularly daring and decided to take Sunshine with us.

Frances, owner of The Bookcase, gave us her usual warm greeting as we entered the store. Cindy, also a regular at our store, came in shortly after Mitzy and I. We all quietly searched for our books in the pleasant silence of the store. By now I had become overconfident and completely sure that Sunshine would remain undetected by other people. Imagine my shock when a string of loud constant peeps erupted from my sweater into the stillness of the store!

Mitzy's immediate reaction was to burst into an hysterical giggling fit then hurry to hide in the next aisle while clamping her hand over her mouth. I stood there hoping against hope that no one had heard, then felt the blood drain from my face as I saw Frances and Cindy staring directly at me.

Cindy spoke first, "What is that you've got?" she asked. Frances was showing the beginnings of a smile, so I felt easier about coming clean and hoped neither would be offended my by little creature. Explaining as best I could about Sunshine and how our relationship came about, then showing her to Frances and Cindy ended up being a real treat. They enjoyed looking at her and learning a little about bats just as much as I enjoyed sharing her. Cindy, whose children attended a local Christian school, suggested that the school children might enjoy learning about bats and seeing Sunshine. I agreed to give it a try. We set a date for two weeks away.

Having never spoken in public, I was quite nervous. My comforting thought was that at least I'd be speaking to children — except for the teachers. Not being an authority on bats, I knew I couldn't give an expert speech, but I could show how sweet bats can be, and explain that they aren't filthy or vicious but are in fact our friends. I earnestly wanted to destroy the misconceptions about bats.

The only information available to me about bats was the one book that the library had. A few other books on wild or nocturnal animals offered a page or two, but the information was sketchy. One outdated book even went as far as saying that all bats carried rabies and should be destroyed. Again I checked out the only book that had helped me so much from the beginning — *The World of Bats* by Nina Leen. I was grateful that the library had at least one book that cast bats in a favorable light. If not, I probably would have destroyed Sunshine.

Thinking back, the whole situation with Sunshine was uncanny. There I was, not knowing or even caring to know anything about bats when I found her, and now the subject fascinated me. Sunshine had lit a needed spark in my life, and now I welcomed the opportunity to actually help change attitudes about bats. The biggest irony was how smooth everything had gone so far. The only "nice" book the library had on bats just happened to be the one I checked out. My father just happening to have mealworms even though we had no idea what they were, then finding a place to actually order them—everything seemed to be happening as if it were all planned out.

That evening, with the book beside me, I started to write my speech. Three days later I had a mere two paragraphs written. Practicing in front of the mirror made me feel like an idiot. The entire speech lasted all of thirty seconds. The kids sure weren't going to get bored—I'd be in and out so fast they probably wouldn't even realize I'd been there. Seeing my frustration, my friend Karl offered his help, and together we came up with a longer speech. I rehearsed with Karl as my audience until I had it down pat. Since it wouldn't be feasible to haul Sunshine's big box from room to room, I used a smaller box that would be easy to carry. Wanting it to be comfortable for her, I did the usual "wall-papering" routine of burlap and stuffed animal ears, then cut a window on one side and affixed screen over it so she could see out and get plenty of air. The only thing that spoiled the effect was the word "carburetor" printed in block letters on the sides of the box. Amateur I was, and I would certainly look the part.

A lady from the office took me to the first class, consisting mainly of kindergartners. The children knew what was coming and were all pretty excited. As I began my prepared speech and got to the part where I introduced Sunshine, the children were starting to get up out of their seats for a better look. By the time I had her out of the box and hanging from my hand, they were crowded around me, asking questions all at once and scrambling to see. The teacher took control and the children formed a line so each could get a good look. So many questions were asked that my well-practiced speech was entirely forgotten.

Sunshine actually seemed to enjoy the attention. The children wanted to pet her, but I hadn't planned on letting anyone touch her. I finally consented to let a few children pet her head, as long as I held their hand and guided them in the petting. Sunshine reacted very well, sniffing and nuzzling a few fingers and graciously accepting the many strokes on her tiny head.

All together we visited about six classrooms. Everything was wrapped up within an hour, but as I was headed out of the last classroom, the twelfth grade biology teacher approached me about showing Sunshine to her class. Feeling anxious about speaking to an older age group, I nevertheless agreed because the morning had gone so favorably. The seniors weren't quite as captive an audience, and I heard a few wisecracks as I was speaking. This made me nervous, but then I noticed two girls who seemed sincerely interested. Thankful and concentrating solely on them, I was able to continue unabated. The questions started up when I finished talking. One of the students asked, "Do all bats live in caves?" Immediately one of the other students shot back, "No way, man, they live in carburetor boxes!" Even I could appreciate the humor in this, and laughed along with everyone else. Sunshine once again won everyone over as they got a closer look. I prepared to leave again feeling even better than before.

It was close to noon and some of the classes were filing into the lunchroom. Passing me in the hall as I was leaving, some of the children exclaimed, "There's Bat Lady again!" "There goes that cute little bat!" I was feeling rather proud of the positive influence Sunshine had brought on the kids. I was also surprised and relieved that everyone, adults included, seemed to have an open mind and genuine desire to learn more about these little, misunderstood creatures.

I was almost out the door when another lady from the office stopped me.

Her voice thick with distaste, she asked, "Why do you have a bat?" It looked like I was finally up against what I had feared the most.

I attempted to explain how I had found her injured and that I didn't actually "have" her on purpose. Offering to show Sunshine to her only repelled her further. Trying a different angle on her, I told her how beneficial bats were to our environment, but to no avail. Disgust was written all over her face, and I knew I would never get through to her. I grudgingly gave up trying and left.

Sunshine was irritated about being kept up all morning and gratefully entered her box when we got home. All in all, it was a pretty good morning as I had accomplished much more than I set out to do. Though the one bad reaction did bother me, it also served to make me even more determined to prove the truth about bats.

eight

ONE MORNING ABOUT a month later my mother called me and excitedly said, "Quick, turn the TV on!" Snapping on the set, I watched in amazement to learn there was an organization called Bat Conservation International located in Austin, Texas.

To think that after five months of finding out everything the hard way with Sunshine, that help was now just a phone call away. After getting their phone number, I happily called BCI, loaded with questions about my little bat.

Everyone I spoke with was extremely helpful. After relating my story about Sunshine and describing her wing injury, I was told that it was very possible she would fly again. If indeed she did fly by spring, I was advised to keep her a few weeks and let her fly around in the house to lose any extra weight she gained and be in shape enough to catch her own food. She probably would have no trouble re-adapting, and no, probably wouldn't return to see me as I had sentimentally hoped.

They offered to send me more information on bats which I gratefully accepted. I hung up, vastly relieved I had found them but saddened at the thought of Sunshine leaving. It would be enjoyable to see her flying around the house, but

I didn't relish the thought of not knowing where her droppings would land. When and if the time came, I guessed I could always follow her around with a mini-vac. Even though I sincerely wanted her to have a normal life, deep down I hoped she wouldn't want to leave. At one time or another we all wonder just what life holds in store for us, but I never thought I'd be a slave to a bat, with a mini-vac in hand.

A few days later the much-welcomed information came from BCI along with a catalog that actually offered bat products. I received two pamphlets full of information that I couldn't seem to read fast enough. BCI was formed because some species of bats are already extinct, and many more are endangered. Bats reproduce very slowly — usually only one newborn per year. Most colonies are quite large and can be easily destroyed, and unfortunately human misconceptions have killed countless thousands. In the U.S., one bat colony dropped from 30 million in 1963 to only 30,000 in just six years. This 99.9% decline leaves 350,000 pounds of insects uneaten nightly — from just one colony. If bats were to become extinct, the consequences could seriously threaten our environment.

Besides being of such ecological importance, bats are also being used in research to help the blind. They are contributing to the development of navigational aids because of their highly sophisticated sonar. Bats are exceptionally long-lived (even exceeding thirty years) and are disease-resistant. Since they can become torpid at any time, they are increasingly sought for research to a better understanding of low temperature surgical procedures. Other contributions include birth control, vaccine production and drug testing.

Bats also form large nursery colonies where all the young stay together until they learn to fly. Despite the vast cave area covered with bats, a mother manages the incredible feat of picking out her own baby's voice from the hungry cries of thousands around it. Mother bats will even adopt orphans when necessary. No wonder Sunshine possessed so many human qualities.

Extermination is one of the major threats to bat survival. Poisoning bats creates far more problems than are solved. Most toxins that are lethal to bats are harmful to humans also, and they rarely kill all the bats anyway. Many homeowners who have found bats to be a nuisance have found exclusion to be the answer. When a large colony is found in an attic or wallspace, the only safe permanent solution is to exclude them by finding and sealing all roost entrances. If a home owner prefers not having bats in their attic, but appreciates the insect control they provide, bat houses can be built (see p. 87) or are available in the BCI catalog.

Tens of thousands of bat caves have been poisoned, blown-up or bulldozed shut, destroying entire caves. In Latin American, poorly managed vampire control programs have killed millions of beneficial bats instead. In Asia, Africa and the Pacific Islands, bats are hunted for human consumption. Hundreds of thousands are harvested annually. In Guam one bat can sell for $25.00, and in West Africa a market hunter can earn $500.00 in a single day. Demand for bats is increasing, but inadequate management has already caused the extinction of some species and many more are threatened.

In tropical areas, thousands of flying foxes are destroyed by fruit growers who kill them out of a distorted fear of crop damage. In reality, these bats prefer fruit that is too ripe for shipment. They may actually help fruit farmers by eating the overripe crop, controlling pests like the fruit fly that easily multiplies in these fruits.

It appeared that bats all over the world, Sunshine's species included, were up against tremendous odds. China was the only place where bats had a chance, where they are considered good luck. Many Chinese adorn their homes with bat ornaments and BCI's logo is from an ancient Chinese design. Five bats surround the prosperity symbol, and symbolize the five blessings—health, long life, prosperity, love of virtue and natural death. What more could a person possibly want out of life?

nine

Sunshine and I settled into a regular routine and passed the time contentedly, both of us satisfied with each other's company. Over the months, she had become almost a constant companion—I took her along whenever possible. Evenings found me talking to her quite a bit, with her chittering back in response; neither of us understanding but still enjoying the conversation. No matter how awful a day I had, coming home to this happy creature—so glad to see me and full of affection—was all it took to erase any dark mood.

Gratefully, I welcomed spring with its abundance of moths. The scab had fallen off Sunshine's wing, leaving only a hint of an injury. She was beginning to stretch the wing out quite often, and flap it rapidly for a few seconds. The other bats had migrated back, and at times she appeared to be hearing them, because she would stop completely still and move her ears alternately up and down. An abandoned ice factory a few blocks from my house harbored many bats each summer, so no doubt she was hearing them. I often wondered if she missed being with her kind, and maybe this was one reason for her "exercising" her wing so often. All indications pointed towards her leaving soon, and I knew I would miss her immensely.

One morning as I was getting her out of her box, I noticed her little body felt different somehow when she climbed on by fingers. I sat her on the bed to see what was wrong. Seeing no noticeable difference I gently started to pick her up again, then stopped dead in my tracks, staring in horror. One wing was hanging limply at her side.

"No, it can't be broken!" I thought, "How can it possibly be broken?" Searching for answers in my mind, I tried to remain calm, but all I could think of were the dreaded words I had read in the library book, "Bats that have broken wings do not survive, they soon go into shock and die."

With her still sitting on the bed, I tried to ease my fingers out from under her without moving her too much. Looking close for any symptoms of shock, and seeing none, I quickly inspected the wing. About midway into her upper arm, the bone was definitely broken. Part of it was protruding almost to the point of breaking through the skin.

Tears were blurring my eyes as I knelt on the floor to face her. Petting her tiny head I pleaded "Sunshine, please don't die, I'll take care of you, just please don't die." Wanting to do anything to keep her from going into shock, I willed her to understand my words.

Even in her condition, she still started towards me, trying to crawl onto my fingers. Thinking maybe she knew she was dying and wanted to die in my hand, I gently tried to gather her up. Even though I did so as carefully as I could, her wing still flopped uselessly downward. New tears formed as I gently put her little wing back by her side to keep the bone from breaking through.

Holding her still in my hand I tried to think of anything

that could be done to save her. The nearest vet was just a few blocks from my house and for now my only hope. Afraid I couldn't drive and hold her still enough, I dialed my mother. While waiting for her I kept checking Sunshine, but she appeared perfectly normal, even chittering to me a few times. I had no idea how long it would take for her to go into shock, or if the vet could do anything to help. Normally my emotions are in control, but this time I couldn't seem to stop the tears. I knew I needed to get myself together to have even a chance of getting the vet to examine Sunshine. I'm sure the last thing he wanted was a blubbering idiot with a pet bat.

My mother arrived and we headed to the vet's. Sunshine lay cupped in my hand, and still looked normal, even yawning a few times and looking around curiously. Grateful that she did not seem to be feeling much pain, I relayed my fears to my mother. She always knew all the right things to say and today was no exception. She pointed out that even if Sunshine did die, I had at least made her happy for a few months and kept her from suffering a horrible death. And she in turn had given me a rare and wonderful experience that few people will ever have. Although her words helped immensely, I still had to fight the tears. My rare and wonderful experience wasn't supposed to end this way. I was supposed to watch her flying off in the twilight, rejoining her kind. That was the ending I prepared to handle, not this terrible thing happening now.

Arriving at Dr. Jarrett's office, I attempted to explain Sunshine's injury to Terre, the technician, while trying hard to maintain control of my emotions. Terre was such a warm person that I instantly felt at ease. After listening patiently, she spoke to the vet in private and explained the situation. From my location I could see her talking to him and could tell she wasn't getting a favorable reaction. I had calmed down somewhat, but fearing that Sunshine might be turned away made me feel so helpless to her plight that uncontrollable tears started falling again.

When he came around to talk to me, he expressed his concern about the incidence of rabies in bats. With a shaky voice I told him about BCI, the misinformation on rabies, and my fear of her dying from shock. I desperately wanted to appear rational, but my anxiety about Sunshine overrode everything. The more I tried to explain, the worse I sounded, and the worse I sounded, the more foolish I felt. The more foolish I felt, the more upset I became, making me feel as utterly ridiculous as I must have looked at that moment.

Still skeptical and perhaps eager to do anything to get this tearful woman out of his office, he agreed to try and help Sunshine. She still didn't appear to be going into shock, and after looking at her tiny little body, a cast was out of the question. Besides being so small, the wing membrane joining her upper arm to her body would be in the way. The only alternative was to tape her entire body, holding her wing close to her side. We tried this much to Sunshine's resentment. She threw such a fit—biting and clawing to get it off of her—that we had to remove it for fear of her injuring herself further. Dr. Jarrett suggested I call BCI and see if anything could be done. Thanking him for at least trying, I tried to quiet my still angry bat and keep her calm.

Back home, I quickly called BCI. They connected me with the Associate Science director, Gary Graham. As I relayed the story once again, I was met with complete understanding and caring. He must have realized how attached I was to Sunshine, because it seemed hard for him to tell me that she probably wouldn't make it. He did offer to call an authority on injured bats and call me back, just in case. Within ten minutes he called again with the same bad news. The only alternative he could offer was to try microsurgery, which was quite expensive. The nearest vet offering this service would probably be in Dallas, and even if I could afford it, I might not be able to get her there in time. He also pointed out that even if the operation was a success and she lived, the wing would always be weak and easy to break again. He suggested the most humane thing I could do would be to put her in the freezer, where she would enter a natural hibernation and die peacefully.

Throughout his explanation, Sunshine was sleeping in my hand and had even eaten some of her favorite, avocado. Over her anger at being taped and back to her happy chittering self, she now seemed normal. I told him all this and explained that I knew it would be for the best if I followed their advice, but I would not give up until she did. She showed no signs of shock, so maybe by some miracle she would pull through.

As far as how she had broken her wing in the first place, Mr. Graham speculated that her wing was probably already fractured or at least injured to the point of being ready to break, and it didn't take much for her to finish the job. There may also have been the chance that she had some nerve damage and didn't feel the injury.

I searched my mind for a solution to save her. If it weren't for the membrane connecting her upper arm to her side, I could easily get a "cast" on her. There was no way to "set" the wing, but it definitely had to be kept still to keep the sharp bone from breaking through. If that happened, whatever remote chance she had at this point would be lost completely. Unfortunately, everything I tried to do moved the bone that much more, and a red spot was appearing on the skin of her wing directly on top of the break. Watching her sleep in my hand in her usual comfortable position, I observed how the membrane connecting her upper wing to her side created a fold when she was at rest. Suddenly it came to me. If I "glued" the membrane together inside the fold with some skin adhesive, her wing would be forced to stay immobile beside her body.

Feeling a slight glimmer of hope, I called Dr. Jarrett to see if he knew about the glue or had any available. He had heard of it, but had none. As we hung up, I wondered if I had given him yet another reason to think me strange. Trying another vet brought some luck. Over the phone I explained to Dr. Immel my entire predicament and idea. He had some of the glue in stock, and agreed to see her. After taking an x-ray, Dr. Immel applied the glue, holding her wing in place until the glue dried. It held fast and was nontoxic. Her wing didn't budge. She seemed to tolerate it fairly well, only occasionally trying to clean it off, but since most of it was inside the fold, she couldn't get to it. All indications showed it working.

All the way home I prayed that it would work.

She made it through the night, eating normally, sleeping and grooming as if nothing were wrong. But by the next morning she had the glue completely cleaned off. Calling the vet once again, he offered to sell me a small container to keep using as necessary. Back home I reglued Sunshine using a bit more than the first time. It held for two days before I had to glue her again.

Being somewhat of a nutrition nut, I had a few vitamin books around. Most of them stated calcium, protein and vitamin C helped to heal broken bones. Since she already liked yogurt, and it contained all these nutrients, I offered her various fruit-flavored yogurt. Peach turned out to be her favorite, so I added a few eyedroppers to her daily diet and also increased her vitamins slightly, hoping that would help.

Two weeks passed, with Sunshine needing to be glued back together every other day or so. One day I was about to reapply the glue when I noticed her holding the wing in its normal position by herself. It no longer flopped to the side! Dr. Immel had said it would start mending in about two weeks, and it looked like it was working! The bone still stuck up sharply under her skin, but it appeared to be slightly rounded on the point, as if the broken end were calcifying over.

Another week and she was almost normal. Although her wing was far from healed, it had definitely mended back together. The bone was not set properly, but the wing was in its normal position and the only evidence of a break was the small knot directly under the skin of her wing.

Gary Graham had asked me to keep in touch about Sunshine. Sure she would make it now, I called to let him know the good news. He was both happy and surprised to hear about how she had been glued back together. It was good to talk to someone who really seemed to care.

By the fourth week I was positive she would be okay. She still dragged the wing, but a new problem developed. Now she was unable to keep her thumb claw from getting stuck in the burlap as she moved around, and once stuck, she couldn't get the claw back out. The break apparently caused her to lose the use of her thumb.

She had become so dependent on me by now that it didn't surprise me at all when she started peeping for help whenever she was stuck. Since I couldn't always be there to "unstick" her, I decided to trim her thumb claw. Her constant "sticking" could easily cause her to jerk or pull on the already weakened bone and break it again. She didn't protest at all when I clipped the nail short and gently filed it smooth. Back in her box she was able to get around much better, although she now seemed more cautious with only three good limbs to hang on with. Hopefully, she would soon learn to compensate.

Sunshine was now definitely here to stay. She would never be able to fly again. Even though I hated the way it happened, I was happy that she would be a permanent part of my life. Whether or not she would become miserable in captivity remained to be seen, but so far she seemed quite content, if not even more spoiled by the extra attention.

How awful it would have been to put Sunshine out of her misery by freezing her after freezing most of her food for so long.

ten

As DAYS GREW WARMER towards summertime, it became impossible for me to wear my sweater. I had worn it as long as I could to enable Sunshine to accompany me "undercover," but it was now too hot for both of us.

For quite some time, I had been entertaining the idea of getting my bat a bat. It seemed this would be the best solution possible. Sunshine would have company through the day, and I would have peace of mind knowing she wasn't lonely. Besides, people look at you funny when you wear a sweater in 95-degree July heat.

All through June and July, I had been walking the downtown area in the early morning hours, hoping to come across another bat. Although I hadn't had any luck, I found it interesting to note the different buildings the bats occupied.

Even in the mid-morning hours, you could hear them chittering and squeaking to each other. A few times, I caught glimpses of bats as they peeked out from under eaves and various places. In older buildings, they would find wide cracks in the concrete walls, and squeeze themselves in to the point of being on top of each other, scrambling and squeaking until they were comfortable. They could be heard clearly as you walked down the sidewalk, and almost visible as you walked by, but as they heard approaching footsteps, complete silence would envelope them, and hundreds of tiny eyes would peer out as you passed.

Knowing not to get too near, I never ventured close enough to disturb any bats. The last thing I wanted to do was cause them to abandon a roost, especially during the day. Nursery colonies were probably among those that I had discovered, and they were up against enough odds without my interfering. I had no intention of taking a healthy bat home just for Sunshine. I knew, unfortunately, that the odds were in my favor of finding another injured bat, and hopefully with my help—and Sunshine's—it would survive.

By now most everyone I knew was aware I had a bat. One morning a fellow storekeeper brought over a small paper bag with something moving inside it. She had found a bat on the sidewalk and not knowing what else to do with it, had brought it to me. I reached in with a gloved hand and gently picked it up. It was a male and didn't appear injured, but looking him over, I judged him very old. After giving him water, I took him out in back of the store where it was shaded and cool, to let him go. But try as he might, he couldn't fly. Since the day was growing hotter, I decided to keep him until evening, so he would be able to find his way to the other bats without having the hot sun baking down on him. I had the sinking feeling he was dying of old age. I thought perhaps leaving him in a cool, secluded spot out of danger's reach would be the best for him. About a half hour later he proved me correct and died, making me wish I would have followed my instincts. I felt bad that he was so frightened when he died. It would have been much easier on him to die in his natural environment.

This was the first time I had seen another bat up close besides Sunshine. I couldn't help thinking about how different he looked from her. He was the same size, but his tiny face was so different. It held all the character of a little old man who had traveled many miles.

The next bat was found right in front of our store one morning, a small female who had injured herself. Her wing was swollen about twice the normal size at the elbow joint. I felt sure she would make it, and excitedly took her home. She seemed scared, but not overly so and was able to eat a few mealworms and drink a few drops of water. This encouraged me further into thinking that she'd be okay. I put her in Sunshine's carburetor box to rest until the evening.

All along, I had wondered how Sunshine would react to another bat, fearing that she'd become too attached to it. If it died, she'd be twice as miserable. I was also hesitant about Sunshine catching something that I'd have no control over. This little bat seemed healthy, with a good appetite and clear eyes, so I assumed it would be all right. I had imagined Sunshine would be excited at seeing one of her kind: chittering, peeping, and nuzzling it like a long lost friend. I never expected the reaction I got.

That evening, I held one in each hand, facing each other. They sniffed noses and acted friendly, but no excitement came from Sunshine whatsoever. She indifferently turned around in my hand—turning her back on the newcomer— to get in her usual upside down position, to start nuzzling my little finger as if the other bat didn't even exist. Perhaps Sunshine didn't think she was a bat anymore, or captivity was more appealing now than being wild.

The new bat seemed to be doing fine. Sunshine helped

lessen her fear of giants, and she didn't appear to be in much pain. She ate well that night, but the next morning she died. As disappointed as I felt, it made me realize how lucky I was that Sunshine had lived through her broken wing, as it was much more serious. The worst break of all would be the long forearm bone. Little did I know that I would soon gain experience in that area that I never wanted to have.

More and more often I was finding bats. Some were already dead and others were injured. Ants were quick to swarm over the grounded bats. Hopefully the bats were dead before the ants got to them. Stray cats in the area were making meals out of those they found defenseless. Each day, it became a race to try and get to the bats before a grimmer fate found them.

The next bat I found was an old female. She appeared fine but weak, and could only fly a few feet at a time before dropping to the ground again. This time, I trusted my instincts, and believing she was beyond help, sat her up high on a small ledge. Checking back later that day, she was already dead.

Later that same day, I found a male whose wing was broken in the upper arm area. Both bones were jutting through the wing, and he was bleeding badly. Feeling he was beyond hope, I did the same thing for him. After knowing Sunshine, it really touched a part of me to watch those intelligent creatures die. Even if they couldn't be helped, at least their suffering would be eased by giving them water and moving them out of the hot sun. All the bats found so far had not survived. It began to look like I'd never find a roommate for Sunshine.

The following Sunday, Jimmy, from next door, came running over to my house all excited about finding a bat in his back yard. I grabbed my glove and followed him over. Laying on top of a doghouse, was a young, scrawny-looking male, probably born just this past spring. After taking him back home, I fed and watered him and looked for injuries. The only thing I could find wrong was the fact that he was so thin. Of all the bats I had seen, dead or alive, this was the skinniest bat yet. In all living things, there are some that just don't get a good start. It looked as if that was this little fellow's problem.

One thing was for sure—he had no problem eating! It took forever to fill him up. Since he was able to fly, I knew I wouldn't keep him. I only wanted to fatten him up so he'd have a better chance the second time out.

After three days he began gaining weight and looking better. He was also gaining strength and absolutely hated to be handled. He ate greedily at each meal, but squirmed in protest all the while he was eating, pushing against my hand with his little feet the whole time he sucked down his food. It was impossible to feed him without holding him, because he'd try to hide behind the stuffed animal ears in the box when the lid was lifted. The eyedropper didn't entice him at all, so it was always a constant battle. He pretty much named himself: Squirmy.

Since he appeared to be recovering and relatively healthy four days later, I decided to introduce him to Sunshine. They took to each other immediately, and Squirmy seemed much more at ease. They snuggled up to each other and slept together peacefully, making me wish I could keep him just for Sunshine's sake. As the days passed, she seemed to be mothering him and I hoped she wasn't becoming too attached.

The next week, I found another injured female. Her wings were fine, but her legs were curled up underneath her, and her back seemed to be hurt, but not broken. She was darker in color, and I had almost missed her, for she had laid in the shadow against a building, barely noticeable.

"Shadow" now had possession of the carburetor box, while Sunshine and Squirmy had the big box. Shadow was the prettiest bat I had found so far. One surprising thing I had noticed was that each bat I found seemed to look slightly different from the others. Not in the body, but in the face. Squirmy seemed to have a boyish but wimpy expression to match his personality. Shadow had a more slender muzzle than the others, and more a deer-like, gentle look. Sunshine was more cute than pretty, with a shorter muzzle and innocent face. The differences were subtle but definitely there. It was astonishing to think that out of the thousands upon thousands of bats out there, each was its very own entity, with its own distinct personality, as different from each other as humans are.

I became immediately attached to Shadow. She seemed unafraid from the start, as if she sensed I wanted to help. She had a good appetite like the others, eating and drinking readily, but much to my dismay I noticed she had blood in her urine a short while later. She looked to be in quite a bit of pain. Her legs were still curled up underneath her, and it was impossible for her to hang upside down. About the only thing I could do to help was try to make her comfortable. After making her a small pouch to snuggle up in, I gently eased her inside. She appeared more comfortable but so helpless that I couldn't help but stroke her tiny head and talk to her softly.

When she nuzzled my fingertip and then lifted her wing to lay it across my finger I was awestruck. I had only found her a few hours ago, yet this wild creature was acting as if it had already been months.

These animals were a constant source of amazement. This was the same gesture Sunshine had once given to me in the beginning. I'm sure it meant something in "bat language," just as a dog will show you its belly, meaning submission in dog language.

Shadow survived the night. The next day it seemed the blood in her urine was diminishing, and she could move about a little easier. My hopes grew that she would live and maybe even fly again if her back injury wasn't too serious. If not, her sweet disposition made her a perfect companion for Sunshine.

The next day she was better still. The blood was completely gone, and she could move her back legs enough to crawl about slowly. She seemed awfully lonely, however. Since I was sure by now that she was only hurt and not sick, I decided to introduce her to Sunshine and Squirmy. They took to her immediately and a short while later, I found them all snuggled up together, sleeping soundly. Sunshine and Squirmy had given up their usual upside down positions to lay prone—one on each side of Shadow, as if to comfort her.

That night Sunshine woke me up with loud, incessant peeping. She hadn't gotten "stuck" in quite a few weeks, but the cry was the same familiar one. I hurriedly got up and went to look, but Sunshine was fine. She was still peeping loudly and staring across the box at Shadow, who was stuck! Shadow had somehow managed to get one foot up on the burlap wall, and had twisted her leg into an awkward position. She was feebly trying to free her foot as I reached for her. Not until my hand was on Shadow did Sunshine stop peeping.

After Shadow was comfortable again, she nuzzled my fingers in seeming appreciation. Sunshine deserved extra attention for her efforts, so I stayed up awhile and brushed her favorite spots—marveling at how special she really was.

On the fourth day, Shadow took a turn for the worse. She had grown listless, had no appetite, and even worse— she was unable to urinate at all. I knew this would probably lead to uremic poisoning and death, but there was nothing

I could do. She felt cold, so I bundled her up in an old wash-cloth and gently sat her on a heating pad. Stroking her small head I talked to her softly, then watched helplessly as she went into shock and died. Even though I'd only had her a few days, I'd already grown quite attached to her. I couldn't keep a few tears from falling for Shadow. On the brighter side, Squirmy was getting fatter by the day. I knew it wouldn't be long before it was time to set him free. If he gained too much weight he would have difficulty flying. Sunshine had grown accustomed to having company; for her sake, I hoped to find another bat before Squirmy had to leave.

Later that same day, a local business called our store. They had a bat inside their building and wanted to know if I could come and get it out for them. I was a little surprised, but glad that word had gotten around so fast about my dealings with bats. At least if I could help, it might save a few bats from being destroyed, and it enabled me to spread the correct information to those who were willing to listen.

Within that same week, I had phone calls from a bank, a restaurant, an office supply store, and a printing office among others. Most of these bats appeared young, so I assumed this was their first season to fly and had just gotten confused and lost. The days were so hot by now that I either let them go in the shade directly under a building that housed a colony, or I'd keep them until dusk and set them free when other bats emerged. What a sight it was to watch the bats take flight in the evening. It gave me a small thrill to let the youngsters go — taking flight out of my hand to re-join the others.

Most of the people that called me had a favorable attitude towards bats, and a few even jokingly referred to me as "Bat Lady." To those who would listen, I explained a few things about bats and gave them a pamphlet from Bat

Conservation International—BCI had generously sent me a few hundred when I requested them. A few people just wanted that "nasty thing out of their building," and could care less about what I had to say. Of course I could easily understand how they felt as I used to feel the same way. Never wanting to force information on anyone, I would just go about the business of trying to collect the bat, but inevitably the question would arise, "Why are you doing this, why do you care about bats?" My usual response was to point out that we are all God's creatures, and besides, just one of these little fellows can eat several thousand mosquitoes a night. As I left I always found a convenient spot to lay a BCI pamphlet, hoping that curiosity would get the best of their negative outlook.

The time had come to let Squirmy go. I still hadn't come up with a roommate for Sunshine, so she'd just have to settle for me once again.

Later that evening, I loaded Squirmy up in the carburetor box and headed downtown. The sun was just setting, and it didn't take long for the bats to start emerging. Picking up Squirmy, I could feel his excitement as he heard the other bats and felt the outside air for the first time in about two weeks. I opened my hand expecting him to immediately take flight, but instead he turned his head around to look at me. Sensing that he didn't trust the situation, I sat him on the ground and backed off a few steps, but again he turned to stare at me as if confused. Hoping there was nothing wrong with him that I hadn't detected, I tried once again, this time hanging him high up on the bricks on the side of a nearby building and backing even further away. It finally worked, and he took to the air, flying somewhat awkwardly at first, but gaining skill as he gained altitude. I watched him as long as I could, but he soon became indistinguishable from all the other bats rapidly filling the air.

As I left, I silently wished him luck and a good, long life.

eleven

Now that Sunshine and I were alone again we settled into our old routine. The solitude didn't seem to bother her as I thought it would. In fact, she appeared more content being by herself now than she was before, as if the temporary company had pacified her.

Since she couldn't ride with me under my sweater, I'd check in on her every so often during the day and take her with me if she was awake. Her nerf cave ended up being her "bat mobile" as she'd go everywhere in it. She'd snuggle up into the dark recesses and happily peek out as we drove off, the bat mobile sitting beside me on the seat.

In the evenings she wanted to be in my hand more often, probably because she was so exposed on my shoulder now. Because of this we discovered an amusing source of entertainment.

Having always tried to be organized, I kept a note pad handy on my desk to jot things down. One day while writing down a grocery list, Sunshine was upside down in my left hand, which I had positioned close to the top of the note pad. As I started writing with my right hand, I noticed her head making small movements as I wrote. It appeared she was following the pen. To make sure, I slowly drew some large circles and sure enough, her head went right around with the pen. Taking it a step further, I capped the pen and went through the motions again, but Sunshine lost interest immediately. Obviously, it was the ink flow, or "design," that fascinated her. It certainly was amusing, and for once I thought I might even enjoy writing a letter!

About this same time Sunshine came up with yet another diversion. Since day one, feeding her had been a messy chore. No matter how careful I was, food inevitably would end up all over her fat little lips and half her face. Lately I had taken to using small pieces of tissue to wipe her face during the meal. This worked out fine, and she actually seemed to appreciate it. So much so that she started doing it herself! In no time at all she had learned that the tissue would clean her face, because she started rubbing her face earnestly against it as soon as it was within reach! From then on tiny little "bat napkins" were a must at every meal for my spoiled rotten bat. I wasn't allowed to use the cheaper quality facial tissue either. Having tried this once, her entire face contracted in surprise from the apparent roughness, and she refused to use it again. So much for pinching pennies, Sunshine insisted on nothing but the best.

As often as I could, I left Sunshine in her box at night instead of the drawer because the box was so much bigger. Her box was starting to look a little frayed around the edges — which was no surprise after 10 months. It was time to get another box or better yet, build a sturdier wooden one.

One night Sunshine took a midnight stroll by herself. I hadn't noticed that her box would be easy to escape from, but apparently it was. Relentless high-pitched peeping woke me from a sound sleep. Right away I could tell the alarming sound wasn't coming from the box. Turning the lamp on and taking extra care where I stepped, I cautiously walked over to turn on the overhead light. I didn't have far to look, for as soon as I bent down I could see her scurrying towards me from under the bed. Her one lame wing was dragging and bouncing uncontrollably over the sculpted carpet, pulling her gait sideways as she ran. Relief flooded her tiny face as she reached my outstretched hand, chittering and rubbing her nose against my fingers in excitement. It was apparent that she had been looking for me. Perhaps I was sleeping so soundly that I never heard her first lonely peeps, and she decided to take action herself, getting overwhelmed in the process.

What she was doing may never be known, but the sight of her running towards me so helplessly will not be forgotten. It made me realize just how completely and totally this tiny animal depended on me.

twelve

Gradually Sunshine adjusted to riding on my shoulder without the protection of the sweater. I worried that she would fall, but her firmly-gripped toes reassured me. At times while cleaning herself, I could feel her grip weaken, so to be extra careful I'd always cup my hand over her until she finished. I would also cover her with my hand when bending over or in other tilted situations. We had come much too far for anything else to happen to her. I guess it was inevitable that she would fall despite my precautions — but nothing could have prepared me for the horrible turn of events her fall would cause.

It happened as I was standing at the kitchen counter one morning, slicing avocados while Sunshine sat above observing her food preparation. I had backed up a step from the counter while wiping it off when I felt her falling. My hand shot up to catch her, but not fast enough. I watched in slow motion horror as her side hit the sharp edge of the counter, snapping the forearm bone of her wing completely in two before she fell to the floor.

"Dear God no!" my mind screamed as I quickly scooped her up. Pressing her trembling body to my breastbone I ran outside to where Karl had just pulled up. Crying out what had happened, we sped to Dr. Immel's. Beneath my hand her tiny body shook, and small distressing peeps told me she was in pain. This was the worst injury a bat could possibly have! Surviving the first break had seemed impossible enough, this time it would take a miracle. The odds were completely against her living, and mentally I tried to prepare myself for her death.

Dr. Immel saw us immediately and quickly assessed the situation. Taking a stick from a long cotton swab, he cut it down to the same length as her forearm bone to use as a splint.

Trying to hold her on the table while he positioned the splint was extremely difficult. She was squirming and biting from the pain, and just holding her tiny body still put my fingers directly in the way of Dr. Immel. Each movement she made caused more bleeding and the bone would slip even further out of the skin, adding even more hopelessness to her plight. After much effort the splint was finally in place and Dr. Immel gently rejoined the two halves of her forearm. After wrapping gauze around the break, he then wrapped a stretchy adhesive bandage to hold everything firmly in place.

Though the situation was extremely grave, I was able to control my emotions. But my restraint slipped away as Sunshine's anguish-filled peeps finally got the best of me. Tears filled my eyes as we readied to leave, when Susan, Dr. Immel's assistant, came forward and offered compassion.

About an hour later Sunshine finally grew quiet and fell into a troubled sleep. Pain seemed to be etched on her tiny face, making me hate my helplessness in her suffering. All I could do was hold and comfort her. So far, she showed no signs of shock and had even enthusiastically taken the small dosage of cherry flavored antibiotic Dr. Immel had earlier prescribed.

She slept much of the day, waking a few times to immediately start peeping with distress. This would continue until she wore herself out and slept again. Bits of avocado seemed to pacify her temporarily, but the bandage tormented her so that nothing seemed to help for very long. Between peeps she would bite and pull at one end of the bandage, or scratch with her foot at the other end. Keeping her from this mission only infuriated her further.

Her eating gave me a small glimmer of hope, but she was so miserable that I wondered if I was being selfish in wanting to keep her alive. The wing that had broken was her good wing, her main means of locomotion. Without the use of it she would be virtually immobile, only being able to use her feet to climb or move about. Even if she survived, there was a good chance that she wouldn't regain full use of her wing. "What a wretched life she would have," I thought, "if she were to get stuck or fall to the bottom of her box while I was gone, and have to lie in that position until I returned." The bandage on her wing already rendered her helpless, and I had no intention of leaving her alone in that condition. Karl had generously offered to "bat sit" for me when necessary, and after talking it over we were both prepared to take turns holding her through the night when she would be awake and in the most torment.

The bandage was posing yet another problem. In her quest to remove her hindrance, she had frayed both ends and was well on her way to removing it completely. All the pulling and tugging on the broken wing was sure to do even more harm. Since another cloth type bandage would never do, I decided to use plaster of Paris.

After Karl returned from the drug store with the plaster, I mixed a small amount with water. While Sunshine was sleeping, I trimmed the frayed edges of the bandage, then applied a thin layer. Knowing the plaster would make her cast harder to remove later, I coated only the areas she could reach with her teeth and claws. Smoothing the surfaces with my finger, I sat back to let it dry and hoped for the best.

Later when she awakened, all her scratching and biting had no affect on the plaster; her teeth and claws slid right off the surface. By evening she calmed somewhat and stopped biting at it and only scratched it with her back foot. Expecting to see some signs of her imminent death by now, I felt uplifted when she ate her usual meal at dusk. But hopes were soon diminished when I noticed the swelling.

Expecting some swelling to occur with the break, I wasn't surprised to see a slight increase in the size of her wing earlier. The cast extended from her elbow to her "wrist," leaving a small area of her wing and thumb protruding from the end of the cast, with the rest of the wing "fingers" folded inside the bandage. The swelling had suddenly increased to twice the earlier size and was growing at an alarming rate. Calling Dr. Immel, he patiently listened and suggested slightly clipping through the bandage to loosen it to keep the blood supply going to the tip of her wing, and applying ice for a few minutes at half hour intervals to relieve the swelling. Finding an area of the bandage between the plaster cast "patches" that she couldn't reach, I clipped a small slit about a third of the way up. Inside, the gauze next to her wing was crusted with blood. Through the night I made tiny ice packs out of an old washcloth cut down to the size of a quarter, with a few slivers of ice inside. The hours seemed endless, my heart wrenching each time Sunshine voiced her misery. By talking softly I was able to calm her each time. In the morning we were both exhausted, but despite my efforts the swelling had actually increased.

Her little wing was now swollen at both ends of the cast, with the thumb end reaching sickening proportions. Not wanting to bother Dr. Immel on a Sunday, I decided to trust my judgment. With extreme care I clipped even further up the bandage, getting dangerously close to the break. The tightness of the bandage had reopened the wound and fresh blood now soaked the gauze inside, making me reluctant to go farther. I clipped as far as I possibly could to be sure it would work this time, and Sunshine actually seemed relieved from the tight pressure. The ice packs were used the rest of the day. By evening the swelling finally subsided. With Karl's help she made it through another night. As the swelling receded further we applied ice less often. Her wing membrane was becoming raw from the cold, so I applied vitamin E to the exposed ends between ice pack treatments. The following afternoon her wing was almost back to its normal size. The danger was finally over but fearing she would be able to pull off the loosened bandage, I coated the entire surface with plaster, leaving the slit area open. Later that day I picked up an antibiotic cream to squirt into the opening to ward off possible infection. Dr. Immel and Susan were both pleased to hear of Sunshine's progress, and we all agreed that it looked like she would make it. The main piece of evidence being that throughout the whole harrowing weekend, the little pig had never lost her appetite.

The cast was to stay on for three weeks. Sunshine was moved to her nightstand room at night, and went to work with me each day. The weight of the cast made it difficult for her to hang upside down, so much of her time was spent sleeping in her nerf cave. After the first week I noticed—with tremendous relief—that she had begun to use her wing again to move herself about—which meant that she wouldn't be miserable and helpless after the cast was removed.

She still seemed happiest when on my shoulder, looking around. Cupping my hand around her I would help her hang on for a few minutes at a time until she seemed satisfied. One day while wearing a pocket t-shirt an idea came to me. By sewing the top of the pocket shut and removing one seam from the side, Sunshine would be able to ride in it. The idea worked well and Sunshine loved it! She could still hang upside down and peek out of the opening just as she did under my sweater. I only wished I'd have thought of it earlier, for it might have prevented her fall.

thirteen

Tᴇɴ ᴅᴀʏꜱ ᴀꜰᴛᴇʀ the accident, I found another bat. This one had a broken forearm much like Sunshine's, except the break was closer to the thumb end. It was a young female, close to Sunshine's age. Although I had serious doubts she would live, I took her home to try my luck at saving her.

She was petrified with fear which made it somewhat easier to work on her. Her wing was swollen indicating it had been broken for at least a few hours, and also making it difficult to reset. After I lined it up the best I could and applied some antibiotic ointment, I copied Dr. Immel's method of gauze first then stretch bandage. I decided against using any kind of splint because the break was so near the end of the wing, counting instead on the hardness of the plaster to hold things firmly.

Up until the plastering the frightened little bat hadn't made a sound, but suddenly she appeared to find courage and started peeping in protest. Her peeps were completely different than Sunshine's, sounding more like squawks instead. Sunshine had been watching the entire operation with great interest from her new pocket, and started peeping back at the new bat. Hearing this, the new bat quickly silenced and peered around, looking for Sunshine. Whatever exchange took place certainly helped, for the bat calmed down and let me hold her in my hand until the plaster dried.

A short while later she was able to eat a few mealworms, drink some water and also enjoy the cherry flavored antibiotic. Her cast was on the same wing as Sunshine's and after introducing them, it was hard to tell them apart. From any distance they looked like twins, but looking at their faces told a different story. The new bat had fatter cheeks, a wider muzzle and wore an almost indignant expression. I later found out that her attitude matched her expression perfectly.

Sunshine and B.B.—named after a favorite childhood taffy sucker, B.B. Bats—got along famously. They appeared to take comfort in each other being in the same predicament, and that may have been the reason B.B. survived. Either that or it was her little spitfire disposition. As the days passed it appeared that they were complete opposites in personality—Sunshine being more of a marshmallow and B.B. being more like a red hot.

Most of the time they would hang cuddled side by side, chittering and rubbing their muzzles together and looking extremely content in each other's company. Occasionally disagreements would arise, with B.B. always being the winner. Since bats rarely fight to the death, preferring mostly to have sham battles, I wasn't worried about their noisy disputes. Most of the time these spats would appear to be over roosting arrangements, both of them squeaking and peeping until snuggled comfortably. It was while observing their comical bickering one afternoon that I first learned bats would hit each other. For some unknown reason B.B. was trying to make Sunshine scoot over, first by squeaking and pushing her nose into Sunshine's side, and when that didn't work, by raising her forearm up and repeatedly bringing it down upon Sunshine's head. This probably wouldn't have been so bad if she hadn't been using the wing with the cast on it, but the added weight caused poor Sunshine to wince in pain with each crashing blow. Sunshine was scrambling away as I reached in to stop the abuse, and apparently my protective action angered B.B. even further, for she immediately turned on me, pounding my fingers and squawking in protest until I withdrew my hand—with Sunshine in it. Unfortunately B.B. was quick to learn how fast she could make Sunshine move with her mighty thrashings, for she used her new knowledge at every available opportunity. Sunshine was also much slower moving than B.B., with her one useless wing and the other in a cast. B.B. on the other hand, seemed completely unfazed by her injury, speeding diagonally and horizontally across the walls of the box with little effort, cast and all. This made matters even worse for Sunshine, for if she didn't scamper away fast enough during a beating, B.B. would chase her down and hit her once again for good measure. Poor Sunshine, her long wait for a permanent roommate was finally over—and she ended up with "Battilla the Hun."

For some reason Sunshine never stood her ground. Perhaps something in the "pecking order" of bats kept her from retaliating. A few times Sunshine would come up behind B.B. and push her muzzle into B.B.'s backside, peeping loudly as if voicing her displeasure. During these times B.B. would tense up and close her eyes tight—looking as if she was getting thoroughly scolded.

During several of B.B.'s attacks, Sunshine would actually get knocked to the bottom of the box. Even though she was climbing around fairly well in her cast, she was unable to crawl straight up because of the other bad wing. Being helpless after she hit bottom, she did what now came naturally—peeped for her giant slave.

After several sleepless nights, I devised a plan for her to climb to the top by herself. Starting at the bottom corner and running to the top opposite corner, I loosely stretched some wide waistband elastic. Securing it at both ends, it formed a two inch ramp. Elastic was used so she wouldn't be hurt if she fell against it on her way to the bottom. The floor of the box had already been thickly padded with cotton immediately following her first trip downwards. Thankfully Sunshine learned fast. By nudging her towards the ramp when she fell and then by coaxing her up the elastic to the top, she caught on quickly. The next three times she fell we repeated the process, with Sunshine being faster to respond each time. The last time I heard her drop into the soft padding I waited for the peeping to start, but heard nothing. Peering in I saw her confidently heading towards the ramp, and after her slow climb to the top, B.B. received a well-deserved verbal assault.

Outside of the occasional bickering, their affection for each other was clearly evident by their constant cuddling and soft chittering to each other. The few times B.B. seemed to be excessive in her abuse, I'd simply remove Sunshine — leaving B.B. completely by herself. Five to ten minutes alone was all she could take. Her sad peeping for Sunshine could be heard throughout the house. Upon returning Sunshine, B.B. would greet her like a long-lost friend — argument completely forgotten.

B.B.'s determined spirit was forever obvious. Like Squirmy, she preferred not to be held while she was eating. When Sunshine wasn't hungry or thirsty, she would simply turn her head away from the eyedropper offering, but not B.B. who would glare at me and literally spit the food back in my face, or blow big bubbles with the water in her mouth. Even when she was hungry, eyedropper feedings were a nasty experience from her constantly slinging her head and food everywhere. A damp paper towel for myself was a must when feeding her, but helping B.B. clean some of the food off her ears and chest would only get me a squawk and a quick hit. We compromised during mealworm feedings, letting B.B. sit in the opening of the nerf cave to eat. At first Sunshine would sit beside her, with me feeding one and then the other—back and forth—like a set of twins. This worked fine until B.B., who ate faster, would finish and then reach over and pull the remainder of Sunshine's worm right out of her mouth. While B.B. gobbled it down, Sunshine would look totally bewildered. From then on, I held Sunshine in my left hand, and B.B. stayed in the nerf cave while I fed them both.

B.B. was getting braver by the day. Feedings usually took place on the desk, with the TV being only a few feet away. Between bites of food she would cautiously peek around the sides and top of the nerf cave, eventually climbing out to explore further. Her first sight of the playing TV frightened her back into the cave. Curiosity drew her back out repeatedly to stare trance-like at the screen until a scene change would scare her back inside again. Before too long the mighty B.B. had conquered her fear, and preferred watching television while sitting on top of the nerf cave during her entire meal.

B.B.'s strong will was at times to her disadvantage. She seemed unable to accept the fact that she could no longer fly, and her pitiful attempts to do so were heartbreaking. Most of her tries were during mealtime. Although I watched her closely, she'd be off in a flash, leaping from the desk top to the floor. After hitting the floor, froglike jumps would ensue, one wing stretched out and flapping. After two or three leaps she would give up and run towards the hand that had been trying to catch her and offer her comfort. As time went on her attempts to fly diminished and finally disappeared altogether. I've always wondered why Sunshine never attempted to fly—maybe she knew she'd landed in the hands of a giant sucker.

fourteen

THREE WEEKS FINALLY PASSED, and it was time to take off Sunshine's cast. Clipping the bandage through the small unplastered slit was easy, but once completed it proved to be of no avail. It would be impossible to open up the cast from around her wing without putting pressure on the newly healed bone, risking another break. The only thing that would soften the plaster was water, so I went to work with an eyedropper full of water, tweezers and manicure scissors. With painstaking slowness I chipped away at the softened pieces of plaster with tweezers and then clipped the bandage underneath into small strips to be peeled away later. Sunshine slept through most of the two hour process, waking every so often to watch over my work. When the cast was finally off, I breathed a tremendous sigh of relief upon seeing the bone healed. The now wakeful Sunshine immediately went to work cleaning her newly exposed wing. Although slightly crooked, she was still able to stretch it out somewhat, and I knew with time it would be almost normal again. Grateful tears came to my eyes.

Two weeks later I removed B.B.'s cast. Her break had also healed, though not as well as Sunshine's. After the cast was on, the swelling must have gone down, loosening the bandage and allowing the bone to move. Her wing formed the shape of an L, with her thumb being on the lower portion of the L. She was unable to fold her wing at her side as normal, and part of it was now splayed upwards. I was grateful that it didn't seem to bother her, but not near as grateful as she was to have it off. Sunshine was perhaps the most grateful of all, with B.B.'s thrashings becoming much less painful!

Throughout the past weeks I hadn't found any bats, but a few horror stories had trickled back to me about people needlessly killing them. One particularly sickening tale was that of workers at a local factory which housed a colony of bats. It seems a few of the brave men had captured a defenseless bat and pinned it by the wings to a bulletin board, leaving it there to die. How powerful they must have felt against this inch-and-a-half-long creature. I couldn't help but wonder that if they *really* knew how lovable bats were, would they still be so cruel? From my viewpoint their act was much the same as nailing a puppy to the wall.

This story and many others compelled me even further to communicate and teach people the truth about bats. I realized I needed to know much more than I presently did, so once again I turned to BCI.

BCI had a list of good books on order, with one particularly informative book by Merlin D. Tuttle, founder of BCI. *America's Neighborhood Bats* includes diagrams and information on how to safely exclude bats from buildings without harming bats or the environment. After I received the book, I made copies of the evicting method and hand-carried them to local businesses, along with pamphlets from BCI. Like before, I tried not to foist any unwanted information on anyone, and was pleasantly surprised that most people were willing to listen and even wanted to know more. During this time a plan was formulating in my mind about doing some sort of bat program for Halloween.

For starters I decided to make a window display casting bats in a favorable light, and blow up some of BCI's pamphlets into poster size to accompany the display. On Halloween Day I planned on having a show at our store using Sunshine, and inviting the public to come. For this I would need to advertise. Thinking a picture of Sunshine along with an invitation inserted into a corner of the BCI poster would look nice, I set about finding a photographer who had no aversion to bats.

Mike Chamberlin's photography turned out to be my best choice. Mike and Carlton, his assistant, had a definite love for animals and after the photo session was over, Mike was affectionately referring to Sunshine and B.B. as "the kids." The best picture turned out to be one with Sunshine resting in my hand looking directly into the camera. Her picture looked great in the corner of the poster, and underneath the caption read "Halloween Special! You are invited to come and see Sunshine the friendly bat."

After tossing out several ideas I finally decided to build a belfry, with bats flying around in it. Unable to find simulated brick material of any kind, I ended up painting bricks by hand on large styrofoam sheets. Once done, large windows were cut out, and black poster board was inserted behind to indicate nighttime. The bell was made of papermaché and painted grey. Plastic bats were to be strung up with invisible string inside the belfry walls.

Without Karl's help I probably would have never finished in time. We started the project in the first week of September, worked on it every evening, painting bricks and modifying evil plastic bats into friendly-looking ones, and finally finished the first of October. The effect was just as I had hoped. Bats were "flying"—by use of fans blowing on them—in one belfry window, around the bell, and out the other window. Strategic lighting focused on a few that were chasing moths. Seeing people stop and read the posters made it difficult to wait until Halloween to give the show.

As the days passed B.B. grew more tame and finally started crawling onto my hand voluntarily. Her taste for different foods grew, and before long she also preferred avocados above everything else. One day I was reading a new book I had found about bats. I came across the statement that bats are triangularly shaped, with the widest part of the triangle being the shoulders, then tapering down to the pelvis. Sunshine and B.B. both happened to be in my hand sleeping at the time, so I looked them over for the triangle. There was no evidence of this shape anywhere. Sunshine resembled an oval and B.B. looked like a circle. Looking closer I'd swear I could see the beginnings of a double chin on B.B. These "wild animals" couldn't fly if they were able to and probably had trouble even hanging upside down. No wonder they always wanted to lay in my hand!

Eating was their main source of happiness which made it difficult to restrict their food. I was, however, able to cut back on their eating enough to rid B.B. of her double chin. The big day was fast approaching, and we were almost ready. Ironically, I thought it was a shame I couldn't dress them up for Halloween.

fifteen

THREE WEEKS BEFORE Halloween I found another injured bat, a small male. The only apparent injury was a bloody nose, probably from getting overanxious in chasing a moth and hitting a powerline in the process. After getting him home and checking him over, I noticed his back seemed to be hurt when touched. Hoping his injuries weren't too serious, I put him in the carburetor box to rest for the day.

Later that evening his appetite was good, and three days later he seemed to be doing better still. I had been keeping him within hearing range of Sunshine and B.B., hoping their chitterings would bring him some security. Apparently it did, for at times all three would peep and chitter back and forth, saying who knows what.

A week later I decided to let him roost with Sunshine and B.B. His back seemed to be getting better, and he was now able to hang upside down. Sunshine greeted him in her usual motherly way, while B.B. sniffed him over, then quickly gave him a few sharp raps to his head to let him know who was boss. Convinced he was recovering, I had full intentions of letting him go within a few days. But a few days later everything I had been working towards was completely pulled out from under me.

Looking back, I realize I should have noticed the signs. Suddenly his legs were worse, almost paralyzed. His appetite waned and he started roosting by himself near the bottom of the box. I rationalized all these signs as something else; until he bit me one day for no reason. With all his might he clamped down on my thumb and started chewing with all the ferocity his tiny body could muster. I felt a cold chill as it dawned on me that this little bat was probably rabid.

The necessary tests had to be performed on him to find out. It seemed to be the longest twenty-four hours I'd ever waited. Since he hadn't broken the skin when he bit me, my risk was not high for contracting the disease. But a rabid animal can be contagious up to nine days before the symptoms appear, which meant that Sunshine and B.B. could have been exposed. The phone call finally came and my worst nightmare turned out to be true. Out of all the thousands of healthy bats in this area, I had the horrible misfortune of coming across one of the smallest percentages around—a rabid bat.

I was informed that I should have the required shots as a precaution, as rabies is deadly and nothing to fool around with. The vaccine is normally only carried by the Department of Health, their procedure being that the patient's regular doctor calls the Department of Health agreeing to administer the vaccine. Only then can the patient go and get the vaccine to be taken to the doctor's office. I was told the shots weren't nearly as painful as they used to be and are usually given in the arm or hip. I was also asked how much I weighed as the amount of vaccine needed depended on a person's weight.

Before I called a doctor, I called BCI knowing what I would be told even before calling, but I was hoping against hope I could do something to save Sunshine and B.B. Gary Graham once again listened sympathetically, then gravely told me that there was absolutely nothing I could do to save them. Since they had been sharing a roost with the rabid bat, the chances were very high that they had contracted rabies. No vaccine has ever been tried on bats, so nothing was available. And as far as the Halloween show, it of course had to be canceled. Part of me could not believe this was happening. How could I have done this to my precious little Sunshine and B.B.? I could only blame myself. But even as Gary was telling me it would be best to destroy them as soon as possible, I knew I wouldn't do anything until I saw the first symptoms appear. I also knew that I hadn't come this far with them to just give up, and that I would try fervently to find some way to save them.

The next step was finding a doctor for myself. Being a person who rarely gets sick, I had no regular doctor. I called every doctor listed in the phone book, even calling the emergency room at the hospital to no avail. It seemed no one was taking new patients, or I needed to be referred by another doctor. Finally, down to the last doctor in the phone book, I found an understanding ear. Dr. L. Singh turned out to be the answer to my prayers.

The vaccine had to be picked up in Arlington, about an hour and a half away. During the entire trip my mind bounced back and forth; from prayer, weighed down by a tremendous remorse at how I could have done such a thing to something I loved so dearly, to relentlessly searching for a solution to save my bats.

Through all these thought processes, one thing kept coming back to me: my weight. Since the vaccine is based on weight, and a person's weight fluctuates daily, then the vaccine couldn't be based on an exact poundage. They would have to give me a little more than actually needed to compensate; just in case I was a pound or two heavier when the vaccine was given. Reading the pamphlets that came with the vaccine swayed me further toward using what was left — if any — of the vaccine on my bats, if I could just find a way.

The next day I went to get the shots. The cheerful Dr. Singh joked and kidded with me about playing with rabid bats, and was extremely easy-going. I had intended to talk to him about my bats and how much they meant to me and using the left-over vaccine on them. All through the previous night I had rehearsed what I was going to say to him, hoping he would listen. After a sleepless tearful night spent with Sunshine and B.B. sitting there in his office I suddenly had the uncanny feeling it was all going to be very easy. After the first injections with the rabies immune globulin, Dr. Singh turned to me as if on cue and said "You're going to have some leftover, do you want to take it home with you?"

For a second I was dumbfounded. Then with my heart hammering away, I recited my story, trying to explain about bats and how much Sunshine and B.B. meant to me. He listened attentively and then, to my amazement he informed me that he also had a degree in zoology, and proceeded to scale the immune globulin down to proportion for the bats' body weights. The amount turned out to be so small that it couldn't be injected with a syringe unless it was mixed with saline solution. He also provided the solution and the syringes and patiently went over the mixing procedure with me twice so I could be sure of doing it right. He said he was reasonably sure the immune globulin would work on the bats; that it would probably kill the existing rabies in their system but was not a vaccine, and would not protect them from rabies if exposed again. He further explained that when a person is exposed to rabies, two different types of injections are needed. The rabies immune globulin and the vaccine. All of the vaccine would have to be used on me, which was fine. I couldn't thank Dr. Singh enough. As I was leaving he told me "That's okay, just remember me in your book." Another coincidence? Just that morning I had been thinking whether Sunshine lived or died, I was going to write a book to tell people the truth about bats.

As soon as I got home I called a neighbor friend Cherryl Cope who had gone to nursing school and explained to her what had happened. Cherryl was also an animal lover and knew about my deep attachment to Sunshine and B.B. She came right over and together we mixed the saline solution with the immune globulin. I held each bat while she gave the injections. B.B. went first because her little rump was fatter. It didn't seem to hurt them as much as I expected, neither peeped or cried but B.B. did turn around to beat up my hand and squawk at me when I put her back up.

The Health Department booklets state that any unvaccinated animal that has been exposed to rabies should be destroyed or vaccinated immediately and kept in strict isolation for six months. Sunshine and B.B. weren't actually vaccinated, and since something like this had not been tried before, I decided to keep everything quiet until I was positive it worked. I decided to wait one year before letting anything be known.

The average incubation period for rabies, which varies greatly, is three to eight weeks for most species. After the eighth week I started relaxing a little. The longest record of a bat living after being exposed to rabies is 209 days. The 209th day came and went with no problems. B.B. and Sunshine grew closer to each other than I ever thought possible, and B.B.'s personality made me love her even as much as Sunshine.

As spring came around again I started going for walks in the evenings. Both bats would go with me, either in my shirt pocket or hanging under my sweater, two sets of eyes and ears barely visible as they peeked out. Many of my walks were downtown in the early evening, which brought us to lighted storefront windows with lots of moths. This was usually their favorite part of the walk, and also became mine. As I continued my walk after visiting a moth-filled window, I could hear greedy little smacking noises coming from my pocket only to be replaced every time by rows of tiny sneezes from the leftover moth fuzz on their noses.

One day I picked a rose and decided to show the bats a small petal from it. Sunshine just sniffed a few times and then ignored it. B.B. sniffed it, then apparently reasoned that it should taste good if it smells good and tried to take a bite. A puckered expression appeared before the bite was even finished, and she then proceeded to angrily beat up the petal.

As the days kept passing I decided to build Sunshine and B.B. a "playpen" of sorts to give them a sense of freedom. It consisted of small hail wire bent in the shape of an airplane hanger, with one end left open. I deeply padded the bottom with cotton batting and a dark blanket. The playpen allowed them to hang freely anywhere from three to six feet high. If they fell, the padded bottom would keep them from harm. They loved it and would hang and watch the goings on—me or the television—for hours. Sunshine was quick to learn about the padded bottom—with B.B.'s help of course. Apparently she decided falling to the bottom was pretty close to flying. One day I was amazed to see her hanging and flapping her little disfigured wings as fast as they could go, then letting go with both feet to hit bottom. Every time I put her back up she would do it again in apparent enjoyment. Before long it became another daily ritual for her. Eight or ten times in a row she would drop, then wait patiently for her slave to put her back up again. When she finally had enough she would stay up and start grooming and preening, obviously pleased with herself. B.B. would watch these little exhibitions with increasing jealousy. Eventually she tried to climb into my hand every time I put Sunshine back up for her next fall. Before long I ended up having to hold B.B. the whole time Sunshine "flew," just to keep her content. B.B.'s distinctive personality traits also included sitting on her hindquarters like a dog, sleeping on her back and reaching out "armlike" with her folded wings to beg for food or to be picked up.

The year finally passed with Sunshine and B.B. always a source of amazement and pleasure. No one can say for sure if the immune globulin worked, or if they were never truly exposed in the first place. I'll always be thankful for those lovable little creatures called bats, and I'm eternally grateful for the pleasure and love they brought me.

POSTSCRIPT

SUNSHINE DIED December 7, 1990. Rabies was not the cause. Approximately one month before her death, the joints of her injured wing became calcified and immobile. She also developed excessive thirst and several other symptoms that, unbeknownst to me at the time, indicated a vitamin D overdose. The small animal vitamins I had been giving her contained a high concentration of vitamin D. Since the body retains this vitamin, given over a long period of time the excess is turned into calcium deposits, which end up in the joints, lungs, heart and other major organs.

Only too late did I realize what was happening. The last morning of Sunshine's life, I found her at the bottom of the box. She was still clinging to life as I lifted her out and helped her onto my thumb. Refusing water and food, she chose instead to stare at me transfixed, as if trying to tell me her time had come. I lovingly stroked her for the last time as she lowered her tiny head onto the end of my thumb and died.

B.B. grieved for Sunshine as much as I. She panicked in the box, searching for Sunshine relentlessly, so I kept her with me much of the day. Small gasping noises, unlike any I'd heard before, would wake me at night. Getting up to comfort her, she in turn would comfort me in her own way.

Gradually life without Sunshine became easier for us both. Through the months, B.B. grew very affectionate, not only to me, but to other people as well. We were invited to schools, churches, Cub Scout meetings and various other groups. As I told people about bats, B.B. would captivate everyone by affectionately nuzzling each offered fingertip and chittering to all.

B.B.'s lonely period ended when Fu arrived. He was found with a broken leg and unable to fly. At first they only tolerated each other but eventually grew close. If males are supposed to dominate, Fu never stood a chance. B.B. never went by the rules.

The last week of April 1991, B.B. turned ill. Her appetite waned, and she grew listless. A few times during that week she tried to pull herself through, with her appetite and affection almost back to normal. Then suddenly on May 1 she died.

About two weeks after B.B.'s death, I learned the diet I was feeding the bats was nutritionally incomplete. Information came from BCI about Susan M. Barnard, a world renowned wildlife rehabilitator. With over ten years experience in rehabilitating bats, she has concluded that only live mealworms and other live insects should be fed to insectivorous bats. Her annually revised booklet "The Maintenance of Insectivorous Bats in Captivity" is available to anyone interested. It can be ordered by writing to Susan M. Barnard, 6146 Fieldcrest Drive, Morrow, Georgia 30260. Telephone (404) 961–4127.

Unfortunately, the book came too late to save Sunshine and B.B. Their deaths were preventable, and at times that seems to be the worst hurt of all. The happiness they brought to me and the respect I now have for their species will always remain, and through this book, they will live on.

Fu is still alive and well, and now has a new friend — Pinoke.

AFTERTHOUGHT

THIS BOOK WAS NOT MEANT to encourage anyone to keep bats as pets, nor is it meant to encourage the practice of picking up injured bats, or any wild animal for that matter.

The bats described in this book all had injuries which prevented them from flying and that is the only reason they were kept in captivity. Healthy, uninjured bats that are able to fly should be left alone to provide their invaluable service to our environment. Disturbing a roosting site or colony of bats could result in needless injuries and even death for some bats. Many will not return to a roosting site once it has been tampered with.

If anyone should have to handle a bat for any reason, a leather glove should be worn for protection. Although bats rarely bite and rank low on the list of animals infected with rabies, the risk is always there.

This book was written in hopes of enlightening the public about bats. Old misconcteptions have caused countless deaths and even torture of bats, when, in reality, bats have always been our friends. Many species are already extinct, and more species are now endangered. The time has come to stop the needless destruction of these intelligent, helpful and, yes, lovable creatures.

BAT HOUSE

Any creature that will eat up to 3,000 insects per night, including many mosquitoes, is a good neighbor.

Bat houses have been used successfully in Europe for a variety of species. The house on the next page was designed by Merlin Tuttle for Bat Conservation International. The exact size and shape are not important except that the entry space(s) should never be smaller than ¾ inch or larger than 1½ inch. Regardless of the plan used, all inner surfaces must be rough enough to allow the bats to climb with ease.

Young bats grow best when shelter temperatures are maintained in the 80–90 F range. For this reason maternity colonies most commonly use houses which provide this temperature range yet do not exceed 90 F. Houses should be tightly constructed or caulked to prevent undesirable ventilation. Europeans often cover bat houses with tar paper to increase solar energy absorption and provide insulation in lower temperatures. Constructing a house two feet tall allows the bats to move up and down to find temperatures more to their liking. Although paint or varnish may increase structure longevity, bats may be repelled until the house is well cured.

Bat houses should be securely fastened to a tree or building roughly 10–15 feet above ground, preferably open to the morning sun yet shaded in the afternoon. Male bats do not live with the females while young are being reared. The male bats may be attracted to a second house placed in a sheltered, similar location. Most bats seem to be attracted to sites somewhat protected from wind.

It is important to note that bats can live only where local food supplies are adequate. For this reason, most bat colonies are found near rivers, lakes, bogs or marshes where insect populations are high. The closer bat houses are to such habitats, the greater the probability of being occupied. Those located more than a half mile from insect producing habitats have a greatly reduced probability of being occupied.

Sometimes bats will occupy a bat house within a few weeks. Often however, bats require a year or two to find a new house. Chances of early occupancy probably will be increased if houses are hung before the last week of July when young bats are starting to fly and explore.

Since the use of bat houses is quite new in the USA, there is much to learn about local bat preferences. Reporting your successes and failures in attracting bats to your houses could greatly add to bat knowledge. Information can be received by writing:

Bat Conservation International, Inc.
PO Box 162603
Austin, TX 78716–2603

Build a Bat House

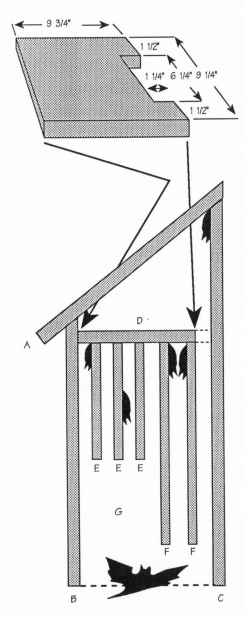

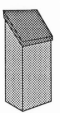

Bat House: designed by Merlin Tuttle for Bat Conservation International combines temperature buffering features and relative ease of construction with the varied crevice sizes most often used by American bats. Western red cedar is recommended for its ability to withstand outdoor exposure, though many other woods are suitable.

Materials: six feet of 1 x 12 inch board and 10 feet of 1 x 10 inch board. (Actual board sizes are normally about 3/4 x 9 3/4 and 3/4 by 11 3/4 inches.)

Construction: overall dimensions may be varied to allow for slight differences in board widths or personal preferences. Spacing between partitions should remain approximately the same. Use rough lumber and turn the rough sides of the roof, front, back, and sides inward. The rough side of the ceiling should face down. Cut 1/2 inch horizontal grooves at 1/2 inch intervals on the smooth sides of all partitions. This will enable bats to climb and roost. Apply a band of silicone caulk along each exterior joint to prevent heat loss.

Estimated Cost: less than $20 and a single house may be occupied by a hundred or more bats.

Dimensions:

A	Roof	16 1/2" x 11 1/4"
B	Front	18 3/4" x 9 1/4
C	Back	27" x 9 1/4"
D	Ceiling	9 3/4" x 9 1/4"
E	Partitions	9 1/4" x 8"
F	Partitions	9 3/4" x 14"
G	Sides	11 1/4" x 27" x 18 3/4"

Partition Spacing: front to back - 3/4", 3/4", 3/4", 1", 1 1/2", 1 1/4"